FAMOUS REGIMENTS

# The Argyll and Sutherland Highlanders

FAMOUS REGIMENTS

Edited by
Lt.-General Sir Brian Horrocks

# The Argyll
# and Sutherland
# Highlanders

(The 91st and 93rd Highlanders)

by
Douglas Sutherland

Leo Cooper Ltd., London

MADE AND PRINTED IN GREAT BRITAIN
BY HAZELL WATSON AND VINEY LTD
AYLESBURY, BUCKS

## INTRODUCTION TO THE SERIES
### by Lt.-General Sir Brian Horrocks

IT IS ALWAYS sad when old friends depart. In the last few years many famous old regiments have disappeared, merged into larger formations.

I suppose this is inevitable; strategy and tactics are always changing, forcing the structure of the Army to change too. But the memories of the past still linger in minds now trained to great technical proficiency and surrounded by sophisticated equipment. Nevertheless the disappearance of these well-known names as separate units marks the end of a military epoch; but we must never forget that, throughout the years, each of these regiments has carved for itself a special niche in British history. The qualities of the British character, both good and bad, which helped England to her important position in the world can be seen at work in the regiments of the old Army. To see why these regiments succeeded under Marlborough and Wellington yet failed in the American War of Independence should help us in assessing the past.

Though many Battle Honours were won during historic campaigns, the greatest contribution which our regiments have made to the British Empire is rarely mentioned: this has surely been the protection they have afforded to those indomitable British merchants who in search of fresh markets spread our influence all over the world. For some of these this involved spending many years in stinking garrisons overseas where their casualties from disease were often far greater than those suffered on active service.

The main strength of our military system has always lain

in the fact that regimental roots were planted deep into the British countryside in the shape of the Territorial Army whose battalions are also subject to the cold winds of change. This ensured the closest possible link between civilian and military worlds, and built up a unique county and family *esprit de corps* which exists in no other army in the world. A Cockney regiment, a West Country regiment and a Highland regiment differed from each other greatly, though they fought side by side in scores of battles. In spite of miserable conditions and savage discipline, a man often felt he belonged within the regiment—he shared the background and the hopes of his fellows. That was a great comfort for a soldier. Many times, at Old Comrades' gatherings, some old soldier has come up to me and said, referring to one of the World Wars, 'They were good times, Sir, weren't they?'

They were not good times at all. They were horrible times; but what these men remember and now miss was the comradeship and *esprit de corps* of the old regular regiments. These regiments, which bound men together and helped them through the pain and fear of war, deserve to be recalled.

Regimental histories are usually terribly dull, as the authors are forced to record the smallest operation and include as many names as possible. In this series we have something new. Freed from the tyranny of minute detail, the authors have sought to capture that subtle quarry, the regimental spirit. The history of each regiment is a story of a type of British life now fading away. These stories illuminate the past, and should help us to think more clearly about the military future.

# The Argyll and Sutherland Highlanders

## A SPECIAL INTRODUCTION

## by Lt.-General Sir Brian Horrocks

IN MID AUGUST 1914 three young subalterns straight from the Royal Military College Sandhurst, of whom I was one, set off from the U.K. to take the first reinforcements for the 19th Infantry Brigade which consisted of my regiment the Middlesex, the Argyll and Sutherland Highlanders and the Royal Welsh Fusiliers; under our command were approximately 300 reservists. After a long journey in those famous French railway wagons bearing the sign 'Hommes 32–40 Chevaux,' we were eventually deposited at a small wayside station. The train would take us no further because no one was quite certain how far the Germans had penetrated into France. So we set off on our own by march route to try and find our regiments. It was my first independent command and I was not quite eighteen years of age. We took all the necessary precautions just as we had been taught at Sandhurst and eventually joined up with our regiments without encountering the enemy, just before the battle of the Aisne. It was during this journey that I developed a great friendship and admiration for the Argylls which has lasted ever since. As our two regiments were in the same brigade we fought many of those terrible 1914–18 War battles side by side. On one notable occasion in April 1917 one Company of the Argylls and 170 men of the Middlesex Regiment after a successful attack found themselves surrounded by the Germans. Although attacked from both front and rear, they held on tenaciously and

Captain Henderson of the Argylls led a counter attack with the bayonet. Next morning patrols found the remnants still in position surrounded by dead Germans, who after suffering heavy casualties had withdrawn. Every survivor was recommended for an award for bravery, and Captain Henderson gained a posthumous Victoria Cross. Some thirty-three years later our two regiments were again fighting shoulder to shoulder, this time on the other side of the world in Korea.

One does not fight alongside another regiment under such circumstances without developing an almost fraternal link, and it is a curious fact that the Highlander and the Cockney have always got on well together.

No good regiment can possibly do well in battle unless their morale is good but in the case of Highland regiments this amounts to something more. They became literally one family. The Sutherland Highlanders are a wonderful example of this. They were embodied at Inverness in August 1800, subsequently they became the 93rd and then the 2nd Battalion of the Argyll and Sutherland Highlanders. In the author's words 'out of a total of 653 men there were only thirty-seven who did not come from Sutherland and Caithness (including the Orkney Islands)'. Roll call must have been something of a headache. 'Ninety-one of the men had the surname of MacKay and sixty were called Sutherland.' The bulk of the regiment shared only a dozen or so names, and in order to increase healthy rivalry within the regiment companies were first of all classified by parishes.

But this alas could not continue for long. Between 1795 and 1806 some 70,000 Highlanders were recruited for the British Army and the Highlands became almost completely depopulated. So, from now on many reinforcements of foreigners from south of the border, Ireland and Wales had to be accepted. But thanks largely to the clan spirit deeply ingrained in the officers and senior N.C.O.s the old traditions were retained and after a few months the newcomers became more Scottish than the Scots themselves. During the last great war the 51st Highland Division joined my corps just prior to the battle of the Reichwald and I naturally went round visiting the different regiments. At one of them I was greeted by a guard consisting of a Corporal and four men all looking very smart in kilts (the Highlanders wore ordinary battle dress in the field). During my brief inspection I discovered to my astonishment that they all came from the South of England. I asked one man whose home town was Newbury in Berkshire how he liked the kilt. 'I had never worn one until an hour ago,' he replied, 'but it seems fine.' There was no doubt at all that the Englishmen were very proud indeed to belong to this particular regiment.

Under the Cardwell System, which linked battalions, on July 1, 1881, the 91st Highlanders subsequently the Argylls (formed in 1796), merged with the Sutherlands to become the 1st and 2nd Battalions of the Argyll and Sutherland Highlanders with their depot at Stirling Castle.

There is no space in a short introduction like this to describe the many great battles they have fought. The author, Douglas Sutherland, has done this for us with considerable skill. The regiment is, of course, chiefly renowned for 'The Thin Red Line' where the 93rd (2nd Battalion), isolated and completely outnumbered, drove back a large force of Russian Cavalry in the Crimea. Although this sterling performance deserved the wide publicity it received, to my mind there were many other operations from which they emerged with equal credit. For instance, the excellent rearguard action carried out by the 91st (1st Battalion) during the retreat to Corunna where Sir John Moore was killed or the superb discipline displayed when the transport *Birkenhead* sank off Simonstown, which resulted in every woman and child being saved though 436 soldiers were drowned. But perhaps the bravest

and toughest operation of them all came during the Indian
Mutiny when they stormed the seemingly impregnable
fortress of Lucknow led by that splendid old warrior Sir
Colin Campbell, who had previously commanded the
Highland Brigade in the Peninsula.

What is also particularly impressive about this regiment
is the number of first class commanders they have pro-
duced; not just brave men who led the battalion gallantly
in battle, but who also cared deeply for the welfare of their
men. To mention only three: Colonel Gordon who served
in the regiment for thirty-seven years and was beloved by
all; Brigadier Lorne Campbell, V.C., D.S.O. and bar (I
am sorry that space could not have been found to describe
the brilliant action in the Western Desert when he won
this most coveted of decorations); and finally General
Sir Gordon MacMillan who commanded both the 15th
Scottish and 51st Highland Divisions during the last great
war and was G.O.C. during the final fifteen months of the
mandate in Palestine.

Let us hope that Douglas Sutherland's stirring book may
somehow find its way onto the table of the Minister of
Defence in Whitehall, because if anything could make him
change his mind it would be a factual well-written history
like this. I hardly dare write these final words, but as a
forlorn hope it might even

'Save the Argylls.'

# *Acknowledgements*

MY GRATEFUL THANKS are due to Lt.-Colonel Tom Slessor at Regimental Headquarters Stirling Castle for providing me with regimental records and histories and guiding me through a considerable weight of literature. Without his help my researches would have been much more onerous and the putting together of the book, including the selections of the photographs, a much more demanding task.

I am also indebted to General Sir Gordon MacMillan of MacMillan of Knap, K.C.B., K.C.V.O., C.B.E., D.S.O., M.C., D.L., and to the present Colonel of the Regiment Major-General F. C. C. Graham C.B., D.S.O., D.L., for reading the manuscript and assisting me on many points.

# Chapter

# I

## The 91st Highlanders, 1794–1818

THE second half of the eighteenth century was a period of great hardship in Scotland and particularly in the country districts. The failure of the 1745 Rebellion had left its aftermath in the breaking up of the clan system and the consequent disruption of a way of life unchanged for centuries.

It was under these conditions that Scotland became the most fertile of recruiting grounds for the British army. Between the years 1759 and 1793, no less than twenty regiments were raised in the Highlands. Young men faced with the prospect of scraping a living from the bare hillside were glad to exchange their lot for the colour and excitement which the army offered. By the end of this period, however, the number of young men available in the sparsely populated area was beginning to run dry.

In 1794 further demands were made on the manpower of the Highlands. The prospect of war with France again loomed large and George III called for four more regiments from the north for foreign service. He appointed the Duke of Argyll, the Marquis of Huntly, the Earl of Breadalbane and Thomas Graham of Balgowan to the task of raising them. They all accepted the responsibility but the Duke of Argyll was in such a poor state of health that he deputized Duncan Campbell of Lochnell to carry out the business.

The requirement was for 1,064 men of not less than five feet five inches in height and between the ages of eighteen and thirty-five. They had to be found within three months. Duncan Campbell set about the task with vigour, visiting

Lorn and Mull himself in search of recruits while other officers scoured their own parts of the countryside for likely men. Officers were, on the whole, easier to come by than men and, indeed, the majority of the men had to be found in the big centres of population like Glasgow and Edinburgh with a smattering of Irishmen thrown in.

By this expedient numbers rose quickly, so that, at the first review of the regiment on May 26, Lochnell stood at the head of a muster of 25 officers, 32 sergeants, 20 drummers and 689 rank and file. Lord Adam Gordon, who carried out the inspection, expressed himself well satisfied with the standard which had been achieved. Although no arms had yet been issued. Lochnell had busied himself with uniforms. The men wore

> 'full Highland dress, facings yellow, lace black and white, yellow oval shoe-buckles, the kilt and plaid green tartan with black stripes'.

The officers wore

> 'Field dress jackets or Frocks, hooked at the top through the shirt. Cloth or Cassimere vests, Kilts or Belted Plaids. Black Velvet stocks (buttoned behind) with false collars; hair cut close and clubbed, well powdered at all parades, with rosettes on the clubs. The colour of the Epaulette white, with facings yellow'.

For both officers and men the kilt and plaid were made in one piece, taking up six yards of cloth.

The arms laid down to be carried were Highland claymores for the officers and sergeants worn slung over the back in the old Scottish way, while officers in addition carried pistols in the belt. The rank and file had flint-lock muskets (known as fire-locks) which were brightly polished. It was not until 1816 that the practice of polishing muskets and bayonets was discontinued.

By the beginning of June, four months after the first order to raise the regiment had been given, they were under orders to proceed to Guernsey. They left Stirling for Leith, where they embarked for Southampton on June 16. The voyage lasted over a fortnight and the transports were so overcrowded that fever broke out, from which one man died. Even after they arrived permission to disembark was not given until July 23. In the meantime, on July 9, the regiment had been officially placed on the establishment as the 98th Regiment of Foot and the officers' commissions gazetted. The reason for the delay in gazetting had been due to the Commander-in-Chief, Lord Amherst, losing the original list of officers given to him by the Duke of Argyll.

Once on shore a rigorous course of training was undertaken to prepare them for overseas service, but it was sadly interrupted by a continuation of the epidemic which had taken hold during their long confinement on board ship. Several more men died, and six months later there were still 137 in sick quarters and 5 in hospital. Living conditions were appalling. There was only accommodation for about 20,000 soldiers in barracks in England; the rest, including the 98th, were either in wooden huts without fireplaces or under canvas. The luckier ones were in billets, although it meant paying fourpence a day out of their pay of sixpence for sustenance.

On May 5, 1795, the regiment embarked at Spithead for the Cape of Good Hope. They must have been glad that their training period was over. They were part of an expedition under Sir Alured Clarke, fitted out to win the Cape for the Dutch, who were allies of the French. The voyage, made for some reason via South America, lasted four months and they arrived at Simon's Bay to find that an advance party under General Craig had already forced a landing.

The show of strength by Sir Alured Clarke's force of 4,500 men was enough to take the heart out of the burghers, who started to melt away. By the time the 98th were ready for action there was practically no resistance and they suffered casualties of only four wounded. On the sixteenth an armistice was signed. The Dutch marched out of the Castle and the 98th marched into what was to be their home for the next seven years.

Although the British occupied the Cape with garrisons in outlying districts, the situation was by no means settled. The Dutch were restless and there were constant rumours of an expedition from Holland to regain their Colony. The 98th spent the summer and the following winter in routine duties and drilling. It was during this time that they lost the kilt. The regiment was ordered to adopt the dress of the India corps – a red jacket, white trousers, half gaiters and a round felt hat. As may be imagined, this caused considerable dissatisfaction amongst officers and men, who had already acquired a considerable *esprit de corps*.

In the spring the first firm news came of a Dutch expedition to recapture the Cape. Reinforcements arrived from home so that when, in August, the Dutch fleet appeared off Saldanha Bay, they faced a formidable task. At the same time Admiral Elphinstone put to sea with his fleet to cut off the Dutch retreat. Faced with this show of strength the Dutch, under Admiral Lucas, mildly surrendered without a shot being fired. To the fury of the troops, including the 98th, all the prize-money went to the Navy.

There followed a further period of routine garrison duty, during which they conducted themselves to the general satisfaction of all concerned, so that on June 19, 1797 the following order was issued:

> 'Major-General Dundas is perfectly satisfied with the attention of the officers and the steadiness of the men of the regiment, as well as the general appearance of the regiment at the review this morning, and returns thanks to Brigadier-General Campbell and Lieutenant-Colonel King for the attention that they appear to have shown on the occasion, as well as at all other times, in disciplining and perfecting their regiment.'

The same could not be said of the Navy, who shortly afterwards mutinied in Simonstown Bay. It was the 98th who were hurried there to protect the town from the mutinous sailors.

Meanwhile an atmosphere of doubt hung about the future of the regiment. There were hopes that they might be sent to India, which was considered much better than the expensive life at the Cape, where a subaltern could not live on his pay. At the same time there were fears that they might be disbanded or drafted, which was happening to other regiments. In the end both fears and hopes were frustrated. There was no posting to India but the regiment was to be kept in service and promoted to being the 91st of Foot, the number which it has proudly borne ever since.

Towards the end of 1798 a fire broke out in Cape Town which destroyed many buildings, including the Naval and Military stores. It was followed by an attempt by some British soldiers to seize the Cape and establish a separate republic. Some of the men of the 91st were approached to join, but they remained loyal. It was partly through them that the attempt was defeated and for this they were highly recommended.

There followed sporadic periods of action like the quelling of the Graaf Reinet Rebellion and the Kaffir War of 1800. During this last campaign the 91st were in camp at Wynberg, the rigours of which are described by Mr. Shipp – one of the few records of the campaign kept by a private soldier:

> 'Here we suffered most dreadfully from the inclemency of the weather, and from lying on damp ground, in small bell tents, added to which our lives were drilled out by brigade field days from 3 and 4 o'clock in the morning till 8 o'clock at night.'

Food consisted of 'a pound of meat (and that of the worst) and three quarters of a pound of bread per diem'.

On May 28, 1802, the Treaty of Amiens was signed by which the Cape was to be returned to the Dutch on January 1, 1803. With the prospect of a return to England, the policy was to run down the strength of the regiment by transferring men to other corps like the Light Dragoons, who were under orders for India. The men of the 91st were unwilling for the

*Colonel (later General) Duncan Campbell of Lochnell. Founder of 91st Argyllshire Highlanders*

most part to transfer but by getting them drunk or by the use of other means of coercion a considerable number of transfers were achieved. At home, Brigadier Campbell of Lochnell was busy ordering 800 sets of Highland clothing for his regiment. To his disgust they returned home only 400 strong.

There is a fascinating footnote about the journey home from the Cape. During the voyage one of the transports was attacked by a swordfish which left its ivory sword, 33½ inches long, sticking in the side of the boat. It was acquired by Andrew Maclean who later became a sergeant-major in the regiment and carried the relic as a walking-stick all through the Peninsular War. It eventually became the property of the regiment and has eight solid gold plates affixed to it inscribed with the battle honours of the Peninsular War. It is carried to this day by the Regimental Sergeant-Major on the anniversary of each battle.

There followed a period of home service during which efforts were made to bring the regiment back to full strength. It proved a difficult task, and the recruiting officers sent to Scotland had little success, although a certain number of recruits were obtained from Ireland. Eventually it was decided by the War Office to form a second battalion to feed the first. By this means and by other transfers the 1st Battalion was gradually rebuilt up to establishment and, after several delays, the kilt was restored to them as their regimental dress.

In October 1805 they were strong enough to join Lord Cathcart's Expedition to Hanover to support the King of Prussia against the French. They had reached Hanover when Pitt died and his successor, Fox, alarmed by the news of Austerlitz, withdrew the force. The 91st took up station in Ireland and they were there in 1808 when they received news that they had been selected to join Sir Arthur Wellesley's expedition to help the Portuguese in their resistance to

Napoleon. With a draft of 264 from the 2nd Battalion they embarked 917 strong from Monkstown on June 15. They then lay for four weeks off Cork and it was not until August 3 that they landed on the Peninsula. On August 11 they arrived at Leiria 'up to our knees in sand and suffering dreadfully from thirst'.

Before the month of August was out, Wellesley had inflicted two severe defeats on the French under Marshal Junot at Roleia and Vimiero. Although both these battles are amongst the battle honours of the 91st, the regiment were part of the reserve division and were not seriously engaged. Indeed, their first real hardship came not at the hands of the enemy but through disease. In October it suffered from an epidemic which put 171 men into hospital and, when the advance on Madrid started, no less than 136 had to be left behind.

The advance into Spain was under the command of Sir John Moore and the 91st were still in the reserve division. By mid-December the British forces were drawing near to their objective when information was received that the French were numerically far superior and, if the advance continued, would be in a position to cut our extended lines of supply. In consequence Sir John Moore decided to withdraw to the north-west. Thus the retreat to Corunna started, and it was to prove one of the finest examples of a rearguard action in the history of the British Army.

The 91st, with the reserve division, now found themselves as the rearguard, in constant contact with the enemy and responsible for protecting the main force. The weather conditions were appalling and rations frequently short. To add to their general discomfort, Sir John Moore had a passion for night marches so that they found themselves harassed by day and without sleep at night. Ensign Ormerod, who wrote a colourful account of the campaign, records how the Reserve evacuated Cacabellos and marched eighteen hours at a stretch to reach Nogales.

'The scenery must have been beautiful, I am sure, had it been day, for fountains in numbers presented themselves, making a waving noise down the rocks; all the way from hence we experienced the most extreme difficulties; without shoes or food, obliged to march, men dropping down through hunger and fatigue – men, women and children in one heap – the Spanish artillery, clothes lying in the road, our horses not being able to draw them up such steep hills and time being precious. At one hill we were obliged to throw away the bags of dollars, which rolled once or twice down and then burst, covering the dirt with their numbers. Our rear was engaged every day. When we were passing the mountains two of our men (91st) fell over a precipice; every ten paces were horses killed ... At Calcavallos (Cacabellos) the Reserve were obliged to cut off their packs, being so closely pressed.'

On the night of the January 8, Moore ordered another night retreat with disastrous results; whole brigades lost the line of march and went astray. Only the Reserve managed to keep their formation and, sweeping the stragglers before it, eventually arrived at El Burgo, four miles outside Corunna, on the night of January 11. On January 13 Marshal Soult, believing that most of the British forces had embarked, launched his attack. Battle commenced in the early afternoon and by dusk the French had been completely and utterly crushed. As Ormerod describes it:

'Towards dark English valour prevailed, when the enemy gave ground in every direction, our men charging and huzza-ing.'

Although the 91st were in the thick of the battle at Corunna their casualties were extremely light but the retreat as a whole had cost them dear. They arrived back in Plymouth 534 strong, having lost 164 men during the withdrawal. By March a further 144 men were in sick quarters as a result of the rigours of the campaign and there were only 337 rank and file left fit for duty.

In April the regiment suffered another blow. The Highlands had been drained of men, making further recruitment impossible. In just over ten years over 70,000 Highlanders had been recruited into the British Army. With the further losses of men due to 'clearances' there were simply no men available and the Highland regiments had to look elsewhere.

On April 7, 1808 the Adjutant-General issued the following memorandum:

'As the population of the Highlands of Scotland is found insufficient to supply recruits for the whole of the Highland corps on the establishment of His Majesty's Army, and as some of these corps, laying aside their distinguishing dress, which is objectionable to the native of South Britain, would in great measure tend to the facilitating of the completing of the establishment, as it would be an inducement to the men of the English Militia to extend their services in greater numbers to these regiments: it is in consequence most humbly submitted for the approbation of His Majesty, that His Majesty's 72nd, 73rd, 74th, 75th, 91st and 94th Regiments should discontinue to wear in future the dress by which His Majesty's Regiments of Highlanders are distinguished: and that the above corps should no longer be considered as on that establishment.'

Thus the 91st, amongst others, again lost the kilt and became an ordinary Line Regiment. The only concession was that they retained their pipers and their designation as the Argyllshire Regiment. The kilt was not finally restored to them until 1864. In spite of the influx of a large number of English recruits, however, the regiment never lost its Scottish traditions and, as late as 1839, there was still a squad being drilled in Gaelic.

The return of the regiment to full strength was still further delayed by their taking part in the Expedition to Walcheron in 1809 as a diversionary measure to help the

## II

Talavera 1809
1 t Bar, likely
some sort of re-enforcements

hard-pressed Austrians. Although they were not engaged in any action, they contracted marsh fever, of which 218 men died. Of the 40,000 troops who landed on the Walcheren, 35,000 were taken into hospital.

In consequence it was not until 1812 that the regiment was again fit for combatant service and sailed once more for the Peninsula. They arrived in time to take part in the victorious advance which finally pushed the French back across the Pyrenees. During this campaign they added the names of Pyrenees, Orthes, the Nivelle, the Nive and Toulouse to their growing list of battle honours.

It was at the Battle of Toulouse that their fighting spirit was most in evidence. Sir George Napier, an eye-witness, described the climax of the battle in these words:

'. . . and then such a roll of musketry, accompanied by peals of cannon and the shouts of the enemy, commenced, that our soldiers were forced to give way and were driven down again. This attack was twice renewed, and twice were our gallant fellows forced to retire, when, being got into order again, and under the tremendous fire of all arms from the enemy, they once more marched onwards, determined to do or die (for they were nearly all Scotch); and having gained the summit of the position, they charged with the bayonet and in spite of every effort of the enemy, drove all before them, and entered every redoubt, and fought with such courage as I never saw before. The enemy lay in heaps of dead and dying! Few, very few, escaped the slaughter of that day; but victory was heard shouted from post to post, as that gallant band moved along the crown of the enemy's position, taking every work at the point of the bayonet.'

Ten days after the Battle of Toulouse, the Peninsular War ended. By the end of 1813 Napoleon had abdicated and been banished to Elba so that, for a while, an uneasy peace fell upon Europe. The 91st returned to Ireland, where they carried out garrison duties and in 1815 were under orders to sail for America. They had actually embarked when news came that Napoleon had escaped and had gathered his army around his again. In consequence the regiment sailed instead for Ostend and occupied the extreme right of the line at Waterloo. From this position they were, to their chagrin, not involved in the battle itself although they took part in the subsequent pursuit and the siege of Cambrai.

There followed three years of occupation duties in France during which time their gallant commanding officer, Colonel Sir William Douglas, K.C.B., died. He had led his men with the greatest distinction through all their battles and his courage and leadership was recognized when he was created a K.C.B. at the age of thirty-five. His personal qualities are shown in a letter written by Colonel Hunter Blair to a friend at the time of his death:

> 'The conduct of the private soldiers from the moment of poor Douglas's death is perhaps the most gratifying and most flattering compliment which can be paid to his memory. They requested to attend his funeral, during which their deportment marked how much they felt the loss they have sustained and after the ceremony was over they expressed their unanimous desire to erect a monument to his memory.'

The regiment sailed for England in 1818. They were to return to France a hundred years later, but on that occasion they were ranged on the side of their former enemies.

# Chapter

# 2

## The 91st Highlanders, 1818–1881

WITH the Napoleonic wars over, there followed a long period of peace. The regiment spent three years in Ireland and, in 1822, sailed for Jamaica. It was necessary to keep a strong force there to control the native population which was becoming restive over the gradual abolition of slavery and from other, largely economic causes.

Jamaica was not a popular station. There were few amusements – even sea bathing was dangerous because of sharks – and living was expensive. Rations were poor, consisting largely of salt beef, and the only drink available was the rawest of rums, which undermined the constitution. Only the really hardened drinkers could find any enjoyment. As one old toper in the 92nd put it: 'It's a fine country; ye're aye drinkin' an' ye're aye dry.'

Worst of all was the scourge of yellow fever. The 92nd, in its first six months of service, lost 10 officers, 13 sergeants, 3 drummers and 254 rank and file from the scourge. The 91st was not so hard hit but, during their nine years' service on the island their casualties were 20 officers, 30 sergeants, 10 drummers and 576 rank and file. At times the strength of the regiment dropped below 300 and reinforcements had constantly to be sent from England. All ranks must have been glad when in 1831 the regiment finally sailed for home.

They spent a year in England and then returned to Ireland, making the journey to Liverpool for the first time by railway train. During this time considerable pressure was brought to bear on the War Office by successive Command-ing Officers for the return of the kilt, but the applications were continually refused on the grounds that recruitment was not entirely from the Highlands. They were, however, still allowed to keep their pipers.

In 1836 the regiment was sent to garrison St. Helena, a barren volcanic rock some 47 miles square, lying in the Atlantic 1,200 miles north of the Cape of Good Hope. Regimental headquarters were in Jamestown, which is situated at the bottom of a deep ravine, while two com-panies occupied the Ladder Hill Battery above the town, which was reached by climbing 699 steps. The only recreations were horse-racing and cock-fighting, but it was still considered to be a better station than Jamaica.

During their tour of duty on St. Helena, the 91st took part in a most interesting ceremony. Before Napoleon had died there in 1821, he had expressed a wish to be buried in France but it was not until 1840 that Louis Phillipe sent a small squadron under Prince de Joinville to reclaim the remains of the great Emperor. The exhumation was carried out on November 14, the 25th anniversary of Napoleon's arrival on the island. A contemporary account reports:

> 'An officer's guard of the 91st was mounted over the tomb. The night was wet and dark, and the work was carried out by the light of numerous lanterns fixed to the trees. A strong party of workmen were employed, and very few minutes sufficed to remove the iron railings and stone slabs, which exposed a square vault filled with clay and stones, under which the body was deposited. By half past three in the morning this tamping, which was seven feet deep, was entirely cleared out, and the solid masonry reached. It took nearly five hours to get through this, so strong was it put together, and it was long past daybreak when the actual sarcophagus was reached.'

Even then the work was not over. The coffin was sealed

in a watertight cell and when it was opened it was found that there were four coffins inside one another which had to be removed before the body was reached; one of tin, one of lead and two of mahogany. The actual body was in an almost perfect state of preservation. Some years later the officers of the regiment were presented with a large bronze medal by the French authorities as a memento of their services.

The regiment remained in St. Helena until 1842 when they were sent to the Cape, which the British had bought from the Dutch. It was an unhappy colony, with the Dutch settlers resentful of the British rule and the Kaffirs constantly causing trouble. At home the Government failed to provide a policy of firm rule to protect the settlers from the depredations of the Kaffirs. Sir George Napier, in his despatches, declared that vacillation was no longer possible

'without the risk, nay almost the certainty, of the plundered, harassed and justly irritated farmers taking the law into their own hands and suddenly entering the Kaffir country with commandos to retake their cattle by force, if not to revenge by bloodshed all their wrongs.'

At this time the demands made on the army both in South Africa and India were so great that additional forces had to be raised in the form of reserve battalions, one of which was the 91st. They sailed for the Cape in the *Abercrombie-Robinson*, which was wrecked in Table Bay. There was only one serviceable lifeboat on board but thanks to the excellent discipline of the men in the battalion, all were safely rescued.

There followed a period of monotonous garrison duty, punctuated by minor expeditions to quell either the Kaffirs or the Dutch. It was not a particularly happy time for the regiment and was made less so by an unfortunate choice of Commanding Officer.

The regiment had always hitherto been extremely fortunate in its commanders, which largely accounted for its fine spirit and general efficiency. The appointment of Lieutenant-Colonel Lindsay from the 78th, however, was not a success. He antagonized the officers and paid little heed to the welfare of the men, whilst constantly comparing his own regiment to the 91st, to their detriment. As one old soldier remarked:

> 'When Colonel Anderson commanded us we had somebody to take care o' us, an' we were men, but noo there's naebody to mind us, an' we're jist a set o' drunken auld deevils.'

It was not entirely true, for the regiment continued to earn high praise from inspecting officers, but morale was considerably lowered.

In 1846 matters came to a crisis with the Kaffirs, who were spoiling for war. In an effort to avert it, Colonel Hare, the Lieutenant-Governor, called a meeting of chiefs at Block Drift. The most important of them was one called Sandilla, who arrived determined to make trouble. During the parley one of his followers was arrested for stealing a hatchet and sent under escort to Grahamstown. Sandilla, however, ambushed the escort and rescued his man, whom he refused to surrender. It was just the sort of incident calculated to start trouble and a punitive expedition was hastily raised which included the 91st. It was an uncomfortable campaign. The British, encumbered with clumsy shakos and red frock-coats with high stiff collars, were engaged against the Kaffirs, who specialized in guerilla tactics and laying ambushes where their assegais and knobkerries could be used with great effect at close quarters.

The work of clearing the Kaffirs out of the kloofs entailed great hardship, but the men of the 91st, with ten years' foreign service behind them, acquitted themselves with great distinction. Surgeon Munro, who accompanied the expedition, praised them highly:

'They could march from sunrise to sunset, and though without food and other refreshment during all that time, not a man ever fell out of the ranks, so great was their staying power and endurance; they never got footsore or leg-weary, for their feet were as hard as horn, and their muscles like whipcord. The only thing they appeared to dislike was a long halt during the march, for their muscles got stiff and would not relax again until they had got quickly over a mile or two.'

The most disliked part of the campaign were the long periods of enforced inactivity while carrying out outpost duty. To quote Surgeon Munro again:

'Only those who served with them and similar detachments at that time, when the war was at a standstill, can understand the terrible monotony and dreariness of such a life. To the solitary officer it was almost unbearable. He could not (at least it was expected he would not) be absent from his post, and yet he had nothing to do there, except walk, listlessly up and down within his four stone walls; indeed it was not safe to go beyond them; he had no one to exchange a friendly word with, no books or papers to read; he had not even the excitement of knowing if there were danger near him, and yet he could not feel certain that he might not be attacked at any moment.'

By the end of 1847 the Kaffirs began to give in, tribe by tribe, and finally Sandilla himself surrendered. Thus, by the beginning of 1848, it was possible to send the 1st Battalion home, leaving the reserve battalion behind, to whom most of the young soldiers were transferred.

The reserve battalion remained on garrison duty in South Africa until 1855 and were involved in the Kaffir Wars of 1850, 1851, 1852 and 1853, receiving reinforcement drafts from time to time from the home battalion. One such draft sailed from Cork in the iron paddle troopship, the *Birkenhead* in January 1852. They arrived off Simonstown the following month, where she struck a sunken rock. The situation was critical and the men were ordered to parade on both sides of the quarter-deck while arrangements were made to take off the women and children in the few boats available. Captain Wright of the 91st records:

> 'Everyone did as he was directed, all received their orders and had them carried out as if the men were embarking instead of going to the bottom; there was only this difference – that I never saw any embarkation conducted with so little noise and confusion.'

When it became obvious that the ship was doomed, the Captain advised the men to try to save themselves by swimming for the boats, but Colonel Seton warned them that, if they did so, they would almost certainly swamp them. Not a man moved. The officers then shook hands in farewell and stood to attention with their men as the *Birkenhead* sank beneath the waves. Not a woman or child was lost, but 438 soldiers were drowned. Their names are commemorated by a monument erected at Chelsea Hospital by order of Queen Victoria and their heroic conduct remains one of the proudest boasts of the British Army. When the German Emperor heard of the disaster he ordered an account of it to be posted in every Prussian barrack room as an example of military discipline at its finest.

Meanwhile, back in England, the fortunes of the 91st Battalion were at a low ebb. They had returned from South Africa seriously depleted in numbers. Recruitment was no longer carried out in Scotland with the result that, although they continued to be designated the Argyllshire Regiment in the Army List, there was not a single man from Argyll in the ranks and under a fifth of the serving soldiers were even Scottish. They were a regiment without nationality, and morale suffered. Colonel Lindsay was not the man to rekindle the *esprit de crops*. When they were inspected in the summer of 1848 by Lord Fredric Fitzclarence 'he spoke freely and sharply to both the Colonel and the Adjutant, and said they must set about it at once and put matters right.'

Shortly after this the Adjutant died and Colonel Lindsay retired. He was succeeded by Lieutenant-Colonel Glencairn Campbell, who had been commanding the reserve battalion and he proved to be just the man to raise the standard to its former high level. The following year they were again inspected by Lord Fitzclarence who told the men that

'during the time you have been in this Command you have laboured under many disadvantages for so young a regiment, but owing to the perseverance of your officers and your own willing efforts, the regiment has obtained a high degree of discipline.'

The following year they suffered an unnecessary blow to their pride. They were inspected by the Adjutant to the Forces, who at once ordered the abolition of the bagpipes, one of the last relics which remained to the regiment of its origins and tradition.

In 1854, after a further period of service in Ireland, they were posted for services in Greece, where they formed part of the Army of Occupation sent there to discourage the Greeks from forming too close an alliance with the Russians. Thus four years passed uneventfully in the Mediterranean before they were posted to India to help stamp out the last embers of the Mutiny. They made the journey by marching across the peninsula to Suez, it being before the days of the Canal.

The regiment was sent to a remote station on the north frontier of the Central Provinces, called Kamptee, which had not been occupied for fourteen years. Not only was it inaccessible but it was completely lacking in proper accommodation. Colonel Gordon wrote angrily that it was 'the most barbarous, the most inaccessible, the most neglected and the most forgotten station in British India.'

Colonel Glencairn Campbell had been promoted to command a Brigade and Lieutenant-Colonel Bertie Gordon, a former second-in-command, came out from England to take over. That the four years they spent at Kamptee were made at all bearable were due to this officer's constant concern for this men. He did everything in his power to establish healthy recreation far in excess of what was usual in the army of those days, when welfare was an unconsidered subject.

Ever since the abolition of the bagpipes had been ordered Colonel Gordon had actively lobbied for the return to the regiment of its old Highland dress. For this purpose he had kept a careful record of the number of Scotsmen, Englishmen and Irishmen in the ranks. Although at the time of his taking command the figures were 241 Scots, 501 English and 323 Irish, he was not deterred from once again pressing the question. He enlisted the help of the Duke of Argyll, who had great influence at Court, and this time his representations were successful. In May 1864 the Commander-in-Chief issued the following order:

'Her Majesty has been graciously pleased to approve of the 91st Foot resuming the appellation of the 91st Argyllshire Highlanders, and being clothed and equipped as a non-kilted Highland Corps. Tunic, as worn in all Highland regiments. Trews, of the Campbell tartan. Chaco, blue cloth with diced band and black braid. Forage cap, Kilmarnock, with diced band. The officers to wear plaids and claymores. The alteration of dress to take place from April 1st, 1865. The white waistcoat with sleeves, issued to other Highland Regiments, will not be worn by the 91st Foot.'

The regiment remained at Kamptee until 1863, when they were posted to Jubbulpore, where they remained for two years before going to Calcutta and, eventually in 1868, back to Kamptee. From there they returned to England in the same year, having done ten years' service in India. Their time had not been served in any of the glamorous stations where a full social life was available. Most of it had been at Kamptee, which Baron Humboldt had described as 'the fifth furnace of the world' and which had an evil reputation for sickness.

Colonel Gordon's efforts to improve the situation are described in one of his letters to Lady Hetherton:

'Under the roof of the Regimental Institution, which, hating as I do all modern affectations of names which are now in fashion, I called by the simple, honest, English designation of "The Soldiers' Coffee-Room, Reading-Room and Shop" was comprised: (1) a comfortable and spacious Reading Room, (2) a convenient Coffee-Room, (3) a shop containing everything that an officer, soldier or soldier's wife could want, (4) a small kitchen, (5) a branch post-office, (6) a spacious games' room, (7) a neatly kept flower and vegetable garden . . .

'The 91st Argyllshire Regiment had a piece of rough barren ground of about 6 acres given up to the Corps as soldiers' gardens. This was a desert in 1860. When I left in 1863 it was a pretty scene . . . my soldiers' gardens were a fair sight by day; but a still prettier one once a week at night. Every Thursday, public orders notified the day before that "the soldiers' gardens would be open for music and recreation at 6 o'clock p.m." I had built a stand for the band and one for the drummers and pipers. A nice shed under which a Restaurant – Cigars, Coffee, Tea, Sodas, Lemonades, Oranges, Cakes etc. Also a spacious round Dancing Floor. Standard lamps on each side of the broad walks. Large numbers of soldiers and their wives and children, officers and their wives present. Glees and choruses sung after the band ceased playing. Dancing got up. The women never joined but the men danced Quadrilles, Waltzes and Polkas to the music of the Quadrille band, and Reels to that of the bagpipes. This weekly fête obtained the name of "Colonel Gordon's Cremorne . . ."

'The 91st Regiment had, or have, armourers', tailors', shoemakers', carpenters', watchmakers', tinplate workers', book-binders', tent-makers' and saddlers' shops. At Kamptee the 91st had an excellent theatrical company among the officers. Besides this there were four other theatrical companies in the regiment – one maintained by the band and three by three separate companies. The 91st had an officers' and soldiers' cricket club for years . . . When I was at Kamptee every company had its football and quoits . . .'

Two years after their return to England Colonel Gordon, who had been in poor health for some time, retired and was succeeded by Colonel Sprot. Colonel Gordon had proved to be one of the best Commanding Officers in the history of the regiment. He had served with them for over thirty-seven years, almost exactly half its period of existence, and was in command during a fifth part of its history.

In the same year as Colonel Gordon retired, the engagement was announced between H.R.H. the Princess Louise

Army Museums Ogilby Trust

*91st Argyllshire Highlanders, circa 1870.*

and the Marquis of Lorne, son of the Duke of Argyll. At once Colonel Sprot wrote to the Duke and requested that the regiment be permitted to provide a Guard of Honour at the wedding. Permission was given and on March 21, 1871, the 100-strong Guard of Honour marched to Windsor Castle with the band playing 'Bonnie Mary of Argyll'.

Queen Victoria granted them the perpetual right to march past to the pipes, but it was also her wish to confer some other mark upon the regiment in remembrance of the occasion. Colonel Sprot seized the opportunity by suggesting that the kilt be at last restored to the regiment, but the Secretary of State for War objected

> 'on the grounds of the difficulty of recruiting for the kilted corps, and on account of the increased expense of the dress (about one shilling per man).'

The next suggestion was that the regiment be designated 'The Princess Louise's Argyllshire Highlanders'. Accordingly on April 2, 1872, the following Army order appeared:

> 'Her Majesty has graciously been pleased to approve of the 91st Regiment (The Argyllshire Highlanders) being in future styled the "Princess Louise's Argyllshire Highlanders" and of its being permitted to bear on its Regimental Colours the Boar's Head (the Campbell's crest) as a device surrounded with the motto "Ne obliviscaris" with the Princess Louise's coronet and cypher in the three corners.'

That the regiment was fully worthy of the honour bestowed on it is shown by the report made on it after an inspection in that year by Major-General Sir John Douglas, K.C.B., in which he stated:

> 'Perfection, of course, does not exist, but although I have inspected very many regiments, I have never seen one so near to perfection as the 91st is at present.'

During their whole existence, the regiment had only

served a brief six months in their native Scotland. In 1871 they were sent to Fort George, outside Inverness, which was to be their home for three years, during which time they twice provided the Guard of Honour for Queen Victoria while she was in residence at Balmoral. It was also during this period that a new system of depots was organized and the 91st and the 72nd were given a joint depot at Stirling.

In 1879, after yet another period of service in Ireland, they were again sent to South Africa, this time to take part in the Zulu War. They formed part of Lord Chelmsford's column which was attacked by some 10,000 Zulus at Ginginhlovo. The 91st bore the brunt of the attack, but it was a one-sided affair. After twenty minutes the Zulus retired in confusion, leaving behind 500 dead. The 91st casualties were 1 killed and 8 wounded. Shortly afterwards

*Officers of the 91st in South Africa, January 1879.*

Cetewayo, the Zulu king, was captured and the campaign petered out.

It was while they were still performing garrison duties in South Africa that a new reorganization of the army took place. One of the effects was the amalgamation of the 91st with the 93rd. From now on both regiments became known jointly as 'Princess Louise's Argyll and Sutherland Highlanders'.

# *Chapter*

# 3

## *The 93rd Highlanders, 1799–1854*

I T is necessary now to go back in time and describe the early history of the 93rd Sutherland Highlanders who were eventually to be 'married' to the Argyllshire Highlanders.

Ever since the rebellion of 1745 there had been a mistrust of the Scottish by the English with the result that a standing militia in Scotland was not considered to be 'a good thing'. Instead it became the practice, in time of national emergency to raise Fencible corps in which the recruits were only signed up for home service and were then disbanded as soon as the emergency was over.

The first Sutherland Fencibles were raised in 1759 by Lord Sutherland and disbanded again after the peace of Paris in 1763

> 'with this honourable distinction that in a regiment of 1,050 men no restriction had been required and no man had been punished (i.e. flogged).'

Six years later it was decided to raise a second Fencible Corps and as the Earl and Countess of Sutherland had died, the application was made to their thirteen-year-old daughter. Her spirited reply was:

> 'I have no objection to raising a Sutherland Regiment; am only sorry I cannot command it myself.'

They were disbanded in 1783 and a third Fencible corps was raised in 1793 by a cousin of the Countess, Lieutenant-Colonel William Wemyss. They saw service in Ireland and were disbanded in January 1799. Three months later it was decided to raise a Regular Regiment from Sutherland.

The task of raising the Sutherland Highlanders was entrusted to William Wemyss, now a Major-General. It was made easier for him by the fact that many of the men whom he had commanded in the 3rd Fencibles, volunteered for regular service. The raising of the remainder was carried out in a way which is probably unique.

For many years the British Government, by various ordinances, had attempted to break down the clan system in Scotland. By and large they had succeeded, but the tradition of clan allegiance remained strong in the north so that, when it came to recruiting for the Sutherland Highlanders

'a census was taken of the disposable population, and the Countess of Sutherland appealed to her numerous tenantry in Sutherland for their able-bodied sons to join the ranks of the Sutherland Regiment as a test at once of their duty to their Chief and their Sovereign, promising the tenantry her protection in all time coming and the provision for their sons on their return home.'

In answer to this call the men assembled at various meeting places and formed up in ranks. Then:

'The Chieftain, or some respectable individual acting for him, with a large snuff box in his hand and an attendant with a bottle of whisky, went along the ranks, and to every young man whom he wished to enter the corps, he offered snuff – the signal was perfectly understood – the young man stepped out, took his snuff and dram, and the clerk recorded his name and attestation. They were then collected and the King's Bounty money paid to them. They were then dismissed to their homes, and subsistence money paid to them until such time as they should be called up for embodiment.'

It was in fact a selective form of conscription but the ties of clanship were such that none sought to disobey the summons. The regiment was embodied at Inverness in August 1800 and given the number of 93 in the Army List. It was very much a family affair. Out of a total of 653 men, there were only 37 who did not come from Sutherland and Caithness (including the Orkney Isles). The nominal roles must have presented some difficulty, for 91 of the men had the surname of Mackay and 60 of them Sutherland, and the bulk of the remainder shared only a dozen or so different names.

The men were above average in height – a contemporary writer reports seeing the Countess of Sutherland in Edinburgh inspecting her 'giant Highlanders' but there was none to compare in stature with Sergeant Samuel Macdonald. Generally known as 'Big Sam' he stood 6 foot 10 inches, in the days when to be over six foot was considered remarkable. He measured 48 inches round the chest and was

> 'extremely strongly built and muscular but yet proportional unless his legs might be thought even too big for the load they had to bear. His strength was prodigious but such was his pacific disposition that he was never known to exert it improperly.'

Big Sam had had a varied career before he joined the 93rd. Amongst other things he had appeared on the stage at Drury Lane as Hercules and had been employed as Lodge Porter to the Prince of Wales at Carlton Lodge. When he joined up the Countess of Sutherland felt that he could not support such an immense frame on his Army pay and allowed him an extra 2/6d a day – a generous provision when the pay of the private soldier was 1/- a day. He died at the early age of thirty-five from water on the chest and was buried in the Strangers' Cemetery, Guernsey, where his grave, maintained by the regiment, may still be seen.

The regiment served in the Channel Islands, Scotland and Ireland before, in 1805, coming under orders to sail for

*Big Sam: Sergeant Sam MacDonald of the 93rd Highlanders.*

the Cape of Good Hope. During this period they earned a high reputation for orderliness and good discipline; it had hardly ever been necessary to resort to punishment. Brought up in a God-fearing tradition there were few men who did not carry a Bible with them and attend church regularly. The men were encouraged to preserve the traditions of their backgrounds which contributed greatly towards the general morale. As the *Digest of Service, 1800* records:

'For in such a regiment not only did each individual feel accountable for his own character but in some degree responsible for the conduct of his comrades; and, as in order to increase wholesome rivalship between the different companies of the battalions they were at first classified by parishes, an arrangement which naturally excited the greatest emulation, it followed that each soldier became speedily convinced that by behaving ill he should not only be covered with personal disgrace, but would in some measure bring dishonour upon the parish to which he, in common with all his comrades in the same company with himself, belonged.'

In 1805 it was decided once again to seize the Cape from the Dutch as part of the new war against their allies, the French, and to secure a revictualling point for British ships on the way to India. The 93rd were part of the force chosen for this task and anchored in Table Bay on January 4, 1806. They were rowed ashore two days later, as part of General Sir David Baird's force, and landed at Lospard's Bay, unfortunately losing 3 corporals, 1 drummer and 33 privates when one of the boats overturned in the choppy sea. General Janssens, the Dutch Governor, could only summon sporadic resistance and the landing was made with light casualties. Later his Burghers rallied and were only dislodged by a bayonet charge by the 93rd. Twenty-four hours later the capitulation was signed.

General Baird, describing the action of the Highland Brigade of which the 93rd formed a part, wrote in his despatch:

'. . . nothing could surpass or resist the determined bravery of the troops headed by their gallant leader, Brigadier-General Ferguson, and the numbers of the enemy, who swarmed the plain, served only to augment their ardour, and confirm their discipline. The enemy received our fire, and maintained his position obstinately but in the moment of charging the valour of the British troops bore down all opposition and forced him to precipitate retreat . . .'

Thus the 93rd first saw action and won their first battle honour.

The regiment remained at the Cape for the next eight years, carrying out garrison duties during which time their conduct was exemplary. Donald McLeod in his *Gloomy Memories* states that the piety of the men of Sutherland sprang from the fact that there were not six houses in the county where family worship was not regularly kept both morning and evening, and that

> 'the early training of the Highlander was round the home fireside. He was taught to revere parents and ancestors, to be faithful to trust, to despise danger, to be respectful to superiors, to fear God and honour the King.'

There could hardly be a better grounding for a good soldier. In spite of the low pay received by the troops the men of the 93rd regularly sent remittances home to help their poverty-stricken families and still managed to subscribe to the Missionary Society and Welfare Funds.

Indeed, such was their piety that, while at the Cape, they founded their own Church (the existing facilities for worship being inadequate for their needs) and paid the Minister's stipend out of their own pockets. The Communion Plate is still a treasured possession of the Sergeants' Mess.

The regiment had scarcely returned to England from the Cape when they were selected to take part in a campaign against the Americans. There had been a long-standing dispute between the Canadian colonists and the newly-formed United States of America, to which Britain, pre-occupied by the Peninsular War, had been able to give scant attention. Now it was decided to send an expedition to the Gulf of Mexico with the object of capturing New Orleans. The 93rd set sail almost a thousand strong and, on December

14, 1814, dropped anchor off Ship Island in the Gulf of Mexico.

There followed an operation which was to prove completely disastrous. A difficult landing was made in swampy ground and the advance started. By Christmas Day the whole force of some 7,000 were ashore and the Commander-in-Chief, Sir Edward Packenham, had arrived to take charge of the action. By the beginning of January they were lined up along the bank of the Mississippi and faced by an enemy under the command of General Andrew Jackson, inferior in numbers but superior in artillery. From then on, due to bad staff work, the disagreement between the Naval and Military Commanders and at least one instance of disobedience to orders, matters went badly. Battle was joined on the north bank of the river with a vastly superior British force advancing against the defending American militia. The part played by the 93rd is best described by Lieutenant G. H. Gordon of the regiment:

'The 93rd moved from its bivouac and advanced in close column. As we neared the enemy's lines day began to dawn, yet we waited in vain and in intense anxiety, for the signal rocket, which was to be considered the order for assault. By this time the enemy could perceive us plainly advancing, and no sooner got us within 150 yards of their works than a most destructive and murderous fire was opened on our column of round, grape and musquetry, rifle and buckshot along the whole course and length of their line in front, as well as on our left flank.

'Not daunted however we continued our advance which in one minute would have carried us into their ditch, when we received a peremptory order to halt – this indeed was the moment of trial. The officers and men being as it were mowed down by ranks, impatient to get at the enemy by all hazards, yet compelled for want of orders to stand still and neither to advance or retire, galled as they were by this murderous fire of an

*The Battle of Chalmette Plain, 1814, where the 93rd suffered 568 casualties.*

invisible enemy, for a single American soldier we did not see that day, they kept discharging their muskets and rifles without lifting their faces above the ramparts, the fire from their muzzles being only visible over the parapets. How long the 93rd continued in so very trying a position the writer of this cannot say, being himself carried off the field wounded . . . I heard a Staff Officer say as he rode away: "93rd! Have a little patience and you shall soon have your revenge . . ." '

The 93rd stood 'like statues' without any orders at all until eventually Major-General Sir John Lambert gave the order to retire. Although the British had succeeded in turning the enemy's flank, the advantage was short-lived. General Lambert assumed overall command from Packenham, who had been killed, and deployed his first brigade to within 250 yards of the enemy. There they lay in the mud until nightfall when, after a Council of War, a truce was asked for to bury the dead.

When General Lambert rode forward to survey his command he found that, of all units, only the 93rd still stood in their formation, proud and enduring but helpless. Their casualties were: killed, 3 officers and 53 rank and file; wounded or missing, 13 officers and 488 rank and file. Of the wounded and missing a further 60 died of wounds.

There was nothing left for the British but to make an awkward retreat. They marched back to the sea, knee-deep in mud. The boats were there waiting for them but they were insufficient to lift the whole force and did not, as had been expected, carry any rations. Thus the 93rd with other units had to wait two days until the boats returned, living on crumbs and without any protection against the bitter cold.

When the force had finally all been ferried to the transports, a new plan was made to attack the town of Mobile. This had hardly been embarked upon, however, when news came that a peace had been negotiated. Thus ended a disastrous campaign.

The 93rd arrived back at Spithead on May 16, 1815, almost halved in numbers but with their honour intact. For many of them their homecoming to Sutherland was a bitter experience. Many Highland landowners had adopted a policy of clearing out smallholders and letting their land instead to large sheep farmers. Not a few of the heroes of New Orleans arrived back to find the family croft swept away and their families scattered.

The 1st Battalion had suffered so severely that they were in no state to take part in the operations in Flanders which culminated in the Battle of Waterloo. Instead, they were sent to Ireland where their numbers were made up with a draft from the 2nd Battalion which had been disbanded. The 2nd had only a very short life, being formed in 1815, sent for a brief period to Newfoundland, and returned to be disbanded in 1815.

There followed eight relatively uneventful years in Ireland. During this period the regiment managed, unlike many other Highland corps, to keep up its almost entirely Highland traditions. At the end of 1823, after a long period away from their homeland, there were only 10 Englishmen serving in the ranks, and 40 Irishmen, against a total of 465 Scots. Thus they had no difficulty in being allowed to retain their Highland dress and the natural language amongst the men remained the Gaelic.

In 1823 the regiment received orders to proceed to Barbados. They set sail accordingly, three companies proceeding direct to Demerara, where there had been disturbances. They arrived to find peace restored but the unusual sight of Highlanders in their kilts made a big impression on the local inhabitants. Believing the regiment to have been sent abroad as a punishment, one negro remarked:

'King George de Fourt was in such a rage and so great hurry to punish dem for deir rebellious conduct dat he send his sogers off widout de breeches.'

The regiment was finally united at Bridgetown, where they also caused something of a sensation. Colonel W. K. Stuart of the 86th Regiment relates the following amusing incident:

'There were a great many Jews in Bridgetown who kept very respectable shops – "Black Hugh" Fraser of the 93rd Highlanders, a perfect giant in size and strength, walking one day into the store of a certain Jew in the town, observed some sacks. "What is in the sacks?" he observed to the owner. "Dubloons," replied the Jew. "Now you are a very strong man, Captain Fraser, and if you can carry those two sacks to St. Anne's Barracks without letting them down you shall have the contents." "Done," said Fraser. The sacks were hoisted on his back and he absolutely performed the Herculean task of carrying them from the store to St. Anne's Barracks without stopping. Meantime the Jew was calling upon Abraham, Isaac and Jacob, and when Fraser arrived at the barracks he fairly began to howl and cry like a child. Fraser kept the dubloons in his quarters and then restored them to the unhappy Jew who, I suppose, never undervalued the strength of a Highlander again! Everybody thought Fraser very foolish to perform such a task for nothing.'

In 1827 Lieutenant-Colonel MacGregor took over command of the regiment. Writing to his sister the following year, Colonel MacGregor relates how he had come out determined to pursue a policy of kindness and goes on:

'. . . but I must say that I have had to exercise but a small portion of self-denial or patience in adopting it, so excellent has been the conduct of my brother officers and so good comparatively has been that of the men. No court martial yet, and our defaulters' list very much diminished. The cause of default is invariably rum – rum – rum – and, poor fellows, they have strong temptations to it, independently of its extreme cheapness. They are induced to drink from the exhilarating effect it produces on their

spirits, depressed by the nature of the climate and frequently too, from the derangement of their stomachs
being temporarily relieved by rum. I acquainted the
regiment that I had two distinct objects in view. First,
that I might see fulfilled in the 93rd Highlanders the
pious wish expressed by our late Sovereign respecting
his people at large that they should not only possess
Bibles, but every man should be able to read his Bible,
and secondly to enable young men of steadiness and
honest ambition to qualify themselves for the respectable
rank of non-commissioned officers, as I was resolved
that the Sergeants and Corporals of the Sutherland
Highlanders should be more distinguished amongst the
other corps of the army by their superior acquirements
and zealous and moral habits than by the rank which
they held . . .'

Colonel MacGregor gave expression to his ambitions for
the regiment by instituting educational classes, remitting
certain parades for soldiers who wanted to improve themselves by attending school. Regimental schools were almost
unknown at the time and the experiment proved a great
success.

The regiment sailed for England in 1834 and in that year
were inspected and presented with new colours by the Duke
of Wellington, the first and only time the famous Commander ever saw the regiment.

'I assure you that I was very much gratified by the good
order, the appearance and performance of your beautiful
Regiment.'

Shortly after this they were again posted to Ireland, where
they stayed until 1838. In January of that year they sailed
for Halifax, Nova Scotia, to deal with increasing unrest in
Canada.

Lieutenant-Colonel MacGregor sailed with his men but
shortly afterwards became Brevet Colonel and left the

38

*October 7, 1834. The Duke of Wellington presents the 93rd High-landers with new colours. From a painting by H. Martens.*

regiment. He had been an outstanding influence and was altogether a remarkable man. He had first been commissioned into the Clan Alpine Fencibles at the age of only twelve. (It was not unusual for commissions to be given at such an early age, but the recipients in their miniature accoutrements often had to put up with considerable ribaldry when they appeared in public.) He had a distinguished military career, seeing service in many parts of the world before taking command of the 93rd. Although he went on to become a full General and to be knighted, his twelve years commanding the 93rd was probably the happiest of his long life. Hodder writes about him:

> 'wherever he went he exercised a singular power for good, and was almost worshipped by his men for his splendid manliness. One fact alone will give an idea of the extent of his influence – when the 93rd, under his

*93rd Sutherland Highlanders, 1852; showing bandsman, soldier and Colour-Sergeant. From a water-colour by R. Poate.*

command, was stationed at Halifax, Nova Scotia, every one of the soldiers used to march to church with his Bible and psalm book under his arm, and it is on record that on one occasion nearly 700 of them took the Sacrament.'

General MacGregor lived until he was ninety-four and a portrait of him hangs in the Officers' Mess of the regiment.

The rebellion in Canada arose through the economic conditions which compared unfavourably with those of the United States and there was a section of the community which was determined to throw off British domination. They were not, however, a very effective force and it was generally only necessary to 'show the flag' in order to put a stop to local insurrections. The regiment spent ten years in Canada, during which time their conduct was widely praised. They were very popular wherever they happened to be stationed, particularly with the Scottish immigrants, many of whom came from their home county of Sutherland. After they left Canada there followed a period of eight years' home service before they were again sent abroad – this time to the Crimea.

# Chapter
# 4
## The 93rd Highlanders, 1854–1881

THE 93rd sailed for the Crimea on February 28, 1854. They stopped first at Malta and then, with the Declaration of War with Russia on April 4, set sail for Scutari, where they were brigaded with the 42nd and 79th Highlanders under command of Brigadier Sir Colin Campbell. There they were inspected by both H.R.H. the Duke of Cambridge and by Lord Raglan, who expressed themselves well satisfied with what they saw.

There followed a period of comparative inactivity which the men found dispiriting. The regiment had been raised to the strength of 45 officers and 1,506 other ranks, and were anxious to be at the enemy. Instead they had passively to endure the excessive heat, bad water and generally insanitary conditions. Not surprisingly, cholera broke out. In the 93rd alone, 416 cases were treated and 54 deaths resulted. It was a great relief for all ranks when they finally embarked for the Crimea on September 7.

By September 20, the French, the Turks and the British found themselves about six miles from a large Russian force who occupied a range of heights in front of the Allied position. The 93rd were in the centre position of the British force and were separated from the enemy by a deep gorge through which ran the Alma River. While the Highland Brigade were still in column they were addressed by their Commander, Sir Colin Campbell, in the following words:

> 'Now, men, you are going into action. Remember this – whoever is wounded, I don't care what his rank is – must lie where he falls until the bandsmen come to attend

him. No soldier must go off carrying wounded men. If
any soldier does such a thing his name shall be stuck up
in his parish church. Don't be in a hurry about firing.
Your officers will tell you when it is time to open fire. Be
steady. Keep silence. Fire low. Now, men, the Army
will watch us; make me proud of the Highland Brigade.'

So the Brigade advanced, led by Sir Colin, pushing their
way through the vineyards and fording the Alma where the
water came up to the men's waists and higher, while under
heavy fire from the enemy artillery. It was only when they
started to climb the steep slope to the Russian position that
the lie of the land gave them any protection, although they
still suffered casualties.

When at last they reached the summit they had their first
good look at the enemy. It was the moment the 93rd had
been waiting for. Kingslake describes it thus:

> 'The exceeding fire and vehemence and the ever-
> ready energies of the battalion made it an instrument of
> great might, if only it could be duly held in, but gave it a
> tendency to hurl itself upon the enemy. In a minute the
> 93rd came storming over the crest, and having now at
> last an enemy's column before it, it seemed to be almost
> mad with warlike joy. Its formation, of course, was
> disturbed by the haste and vehemence of the onset . . .
> But Sir Colin got the regiment to halt and dress its ranks.
> By this time it was under fire of the approaching column.'

The Russians lowered their bayonets as if to charge but
the Highlanders swept irresistibly onwards. Sir Colin's
horse was shot from under him and the Adjutant received a
ball in his shoulder, but the advance did not check. It was
the Russians who first hesitated and then retired in confusion. A captured Russian general afterwards said that when
their infantry caught sight of the bare legs of the Highlanders and their waving plumes emerging from the smoke,
they could not stand firm.

Sir Colin was so impressed by his brigade, that he asked

*The Battle of the Alma, September 20, 1854. The 93rd occupied the centre of the Highland Brigade, with the 42nd and 79th on either flank.*

permission of General Raglan to be permitted to wear a Highland bonnet for the rest of the campaign instead of his cocked hat. It was a gesture which delighted the men of the 93rd.

A month later the regiment were protecting Balaclava, which had been cleared of civilians in order to accommodate the needs of the military. At first light on the morning of October 25 a force of about 25,000 Russians with 78 guns started an advance against the position which was held by the 93rd in the centre and a battalion of Turks on either flank. The first weight of the attack fell on the Turks, who fled after a short show of resistance. The 93rd were in consequence left entirely isolated to face the main charge of the Russian cavalry. At this juncture Sir Colin Campbell rode down their ranks and said to them:

'There is no retreat from here, men. You must die where you stand.'

The right-hand man of No. 6 Company, John Scott, at once replied:

'Ay, ay, Sir Colin, and needs be we'll do that.'

The cry was at once taken up along the ranks.

A large force of Russian cavalry now appeared on the plain at about a thousand yards distant. They advanced at a trot, breaking into a gallop. The 93rd did not change formation but remained two deep instead of falling in four deep as would have been more usual. At 500 yards they fired their first volley which had little effect on the advancing horde. They then held their fire until the enemy were within 250 yards before firing again. This time they wheeled and broke in confusion, to be pursued and routed by the Heavy Cavalry Brigade.

Sir W. H. Russell, *The Times* correspondent, observed the action from 'the Col', near Lord Raglan's headquarters and described it thus:

'As the Russian cavalry on the left of their line crowned the hill across the valley they perceived the Highlanders drawn up at the distance of some half-mile. They halted and squadron after squadron came up from the rear. The Russians drew breath for a moment and then in one grand line charged towards Balaclava. The ground flew beneath their horses' feet; gathering speed at every stride, they dashed on towards the thin red streak tipped with a line of steel. The Turks fired a volley at 800 yards and ran. As the Russians came within 600 yards, down went that line of steel in front, and out rang a volley of Minie musketry. The distance was too great, the Russians were not checked but swept onwards, here and there knocked over by the shot of our batteries, but ere they came within 250 yards another volley flashed from the rifles. The Russians wheeled about and fled faster than they came. "Bravo, Highlanders! Well done!" shouted the excited spectators. But events thickened, the Highlanders and their splendid front were soon forgotten – men had scarcely a moment to think of this fact: that the 93rd never altered their formation to receive that tide of horsemen.'

In fact, when the Russian front broke, it was all Sir Colin could do to restrain his men from rushing forward to try and decide the issue with the bayonet. At the height of the action the old soldier's voice could be heard crying fiercely:

'93rd! 93rd! Damn all that eagerness!'

It was remarked with disappointment by the men of the 93rd after this action that they seemed to have inflicted very few casualties on the enemy and few horses were seen to be rendered riderless. Two years later some British officers were paying a visit to the Russian officers who had taken part in the charge and mentioned this point. The Russians stated:

'. . . we were unable to rein up or slacken speed or swerve to the left before we received your second volley by which

'The Thin Red Line.' The 93rd at the Battle of Balaclava, October 25, 1854.

almost every man and horse in our ranks was wounded
... But you knew, of course, that a mounted man,
though severely and even mortally wounded, can retain
his seat in the saddle long enough to ride out of danger.
If you are a sportsman you will understand that if you
wound a deer or a hare, and do not kill it, it will run a
long way before it falls, and so will a horse; and no
soldier will tumble off his horse as long as he can hold
on, but will cling to it in the hope of its carrying him out
of action, and so it was with us.'

It was this action at Balaclava which earned the regiment
the description of 'The Thin Red Line', which was eventually
immortalized by Robert Gibbs's well-known painting of that
name. The last survivor of the action died in London in
1927 at the age of ninety-eight (Sergeant C. Ellingsworth).

At the beginning of November another assault was made
on the British position, this time on the right flank at
Inkerman. General Liprandi waited with a large Russian
force to hear the outcome at Inkerman before launching a
second attack on Balaclava. By 2 p.m. on November 4 the
result was known. The British had lost 567 killed and 1,933
wounded but the Russians had been forced to retire with a
casualty list of over 11,000.

The Battle of Inkerman was the last of the fighting for
that year. On November 14 there was a hurricane of such
severity that whole trees were uprooted, houses were blown
down and every tent was completely flattened, and the
troops suffered badly from exposure. It was only the beginning of a winter of unremitting misery. Because the roads
were almost impassable for mud and in any case the horses
were in too weak a state for arduous work, the troops around
Balaclava, including the 93rd, were employed in back-
breaking fatigues involving the carrying of cannon-balls four
miles through heavy mud up to the Cheronese Heights.
They alternately froze from immersion in the icy mud and
perspired from the intense exertion. They had no change of

clothing and little opportunity of ever getting dry. The flaps of their tents, for strategic reasons, opened to the north and the prevailing wind. Lying on the ground in their wet clothes they could only look forward to the next issue of grog. Sickness was rife but the doctors had no supplies or equipment to relieve the suffering.

Dr. Munro, of the 93rd, was lucky to have an old church building as a hospital, but even then conditions were appalling. Here is his account:

'The church was always filled to overcrowding, and the poor fellows lay packed as close as possible on the floor, in their soiled and tattered uniforms and covered only with their worn field blankets. Before the end of the winter, boards and trestles were supplied in lieu of hospital cots, but these were not more comfortable than the wooden floor of the church. There the surgeons bravely worked and toiled by day and night with little power and less hope of doing good, for they had only a very scanty supply of medicines and no bread or soup or wine or any single article with which to nourish the starving sick.

'By day and by night at every hour, men came from camp, from guard, from picket and from fatigue duty, wet, cold, benumbed, with life just flickering in their feebly beating hearts; and only warmth and nourishment were required to rouse the flicker into a flame and bring them back to life. But all that could be done was to lay them gently down and watch life ebb away, often without a struggle or a moan. And yet the British soldier, in all this misery, never uttered one word of complaint and was an object to be looked at with admiration and respect.

'During that awful winter ... food, shelter and proper clothing were all that he required to enable him to undergo any amount of labour and exposure, but these were not supplied in time to save many a life ...'

By March, 969 men of the 93rd had passed through the

rough and ready hospital and 88 had died. It was only after the worst was over that large quantities of warm clothing and other luxuries began to arrive from home. Towards the end of the month the Highland Regiments received new kilts, purses, hose and feathered bonnets and, miraculously

> 'looked as grand and as imposing as ever, with an effective strength not much impaired, owing to the arrival of drafts from home during the winter and spring.'

Since the Battle of Inkerman, the Allies had been steadily bombarding and sapping up to Sevastopol. By mid-June the 93rd, having returned from an expedition to Kertch, were in the trenches before Sevastopol when the first grand assault was launched against the Redan. It was beaten back. A second assault was made on September 8, again with heavy losses to the British, although the 93rd were only marginally engaged. Following this, the Adjutant of the 93rd went out to try and bring in some of the wounded and, approaching close to the Redan, observed very little activity. Reporting this, he requested permission to investigate further. A party of ten volunteers was called for from the 93rd, who made the discovery that the Russians had indeed withdrawn. Cautiously Sir Colin Campbell refused to allow it to be immediately occupied. Shortly afterwards there was a tremendous explosion as it blew up.

Although hostilities had not entirely ceased, the Siege of Sevastopol was now over and the more normal routine of drills and exercises recommenced. The second winter in the Crimea was passed under much better conditions than the first. Rations were much improved, accommodation was warm and there was even a theatre for the diversion of the troops. An armistice was signed on March 1 and fraternization started between the Russian and the British armies. Peace was finally declared in April and General Luders, the Russian Commander, reviewed the French and British troops. On May 9, Sir Colin Campbell, who was to embark for home, made this final address to the Highland Brigade:

'Soldiers of the 42nd, 79th and 93rd! Old Highland Brigade, with whom I have passed the early and perilous part of this war, I now have to take leave of you. In a few hours I shall be aboard ship never to see you again as a body. A long farewell! I am now old and shall not be called to serve any more, and nothing will remain to me but the memory of my campaign and of the enduring, hardy, generous soldiers with whom I have been associated, whose name and glory will long be kept in the hearts of our countrymen. When you go home, as you gradually fulfil your term of service, each to his family and his cottage, you will tell the story of your immortal advance in that victorious echelon up the heights of Alma, and of the old Brigadier who led and loved you so well. Your children and your children's children will repeat the tale to other generations when only a few lines of history will remain to record all the enthusiasm and discipline which you have born so stoutly to the end of this war.

'Our native land will never forget the name of the Highland Brigade and in some future war that native land will call for another one to equal this which it can never surpass. Though I shall be gone, the thought of you will go with me wherever I may be and cheer my old age with a glorious recollection of dangers confronted and hardships endured. A pipe will never sound near me without carrying me back to those bright days when I was at your head, and wore the bonnet which you gained for me, and the honourable decorations on my breast, many of which I owe to your conduct. Brave soldiers, kind comrades, farewell.'

The following month the 93rd, followed their gallant Commander home and was the only Highland Regiment to take part in the grand review of troops returned from the Crimea, by Queen Victoria and Prince Albert. The *Illustrated London News* of July 19, 1856 recorded:

*A bandsman of the 93rd Highlanders performing the Sword Dance. From a painting by David Cunliffe dated 1853.*

'With the Highlanders, whose Colours, which were literally in rags, bore testimony to the hard service the Regiment had gone through, the Queen seemed particularly pleased . . .'

The regiment was not left for long to kick its heels at home. In January 1857 they received orders to embark for China, where trouble was imminent. At the last moment a crisis in India caused the orders to be changed and the regiment rerouted there, to deal with the increasingly serious Indian Mutiny. They sailed 1,070 men strong, of whom 25 were English, 51 Irish and 994 Scottish. Just after the ship, s.s. *Mauritius*, had left Cape Town a mutiny broke out aboard; the Captain would have had to put back to port but for the fact that there were so many soldiers of the 93rd who had been fishermen that they were able to supply no less than eight-three men who were capable of going aloft in all weathers, and they were able to sail the ship to its destination.

On arrival at Calcutta the new Commander-in-Chief in India came aboard and was received with rapturous cheers from the men of the 93rd, for he was none other than their beloved Sir Colin Campbell, who had so recently taken leave of them in the Crimea.

The first destination of the 93rd was Cawnpore. Before they reached there, however, their journey was interrupted in order to attack a body of about 3,000 rebels who were occupying the village of Khaga and who, it was feared, were planning to march across country to join the large rebel force which invested the beleaguered town of Lucknow. This was successfully accomplished with a total loss to the punitive force of 24 killed and 77 wounded, and gave the 93rd their first taste of a new kind of warfare.

Cawnpore had been the scene of the most hideous slaughter, on the orders of the Nana Sahib, of some two hundred white women and children, who had been thrown dead or dying down a well. The troops were allowed to visit the scene of this atrocity in organized parties when they could see for themselves the evidence of the tortures inflicted before the massacre. One particularly gory exhibit was a butcher's hook fixed in a wall from which, it was obvious from the bloody marks of baby hands and feet, a small child had hung in its death agonies.

Nothing could have had a more salutary effect on the British troops or steeled them to a greater extent for the desperate task which lay before them. Lucknow had fallen into the hands of the rebels, who occupied it in great force. The British community of men, women and children were besieged in the Residency where they were in danger of meeting the same fate as the residents of Cawnpore. Their relief was imperative but the British force available to breach the strong defences was pitiably small – about 4,000 men – compared with the rebels, who outnumbered them three or four to one.

On November 11 Sir Colin Campbell, who had just arrived from Calcutta to take personal charge of the operation, inspected his force drawn up by brigades facing Lucknow, and made a short speech:

> 'Soldiers! We are about to advance to the relief of our countrymen and countrywomen besieged in the Residency by overwhelming numbers of rebels. It will be a duty of difficulty and danger, but I rely on you.'

The announcement was greeted with thunderous cheers, led by the 93rd.

The attack on Lucknow was fraught with difficulties. Before reaching the main fortifications, the attackers had to fight their way through the outer defences under heavy fire from the main enemy positions. This being successfully accomplished, they were faced with storming the walls of the Barracks and the Sikanderbagh. To achieve this the 93rd were brought to the front under heavy rifle fire while the artillery sought to create a breach in one of the walls.

After about one and a half hours of battering a small breach was affected about three feet square, scarcely big enough for a man to crawl through. At once Sir Colin ordered a drummer-boy of the 93rd to sound the advance, whereupon the whole British line rose and rushed cheering towards the wall.

> 'It was not a cheer, but a concentrated yell of rage and ferocity that made the echoes ring again ... Pipe-Major John MacLeod with seven pipers ... struck up the Highland Charge, "The Haughs of Cromdell", also known as "On wi' the Tartan" – said to be the famous Charge of the great Montrose when he led his Highlanders so often to victory.' – Forbes-Mitchell.

There is some doubt as to who was actually the first to

A.S.H.—5

enter the breach but a small party of nine was soon inside the walls, including Colonel Ewart, Commanding the regiment. One of the stormers must have been a drummer-boy of the 93rd, as an eye-witness later reported seeing

> 'just inside the breach, lying on his back quite dead, a pretty innocent-looking fair-haired lad not more than fourteen years of age.'

The breaching party were heavily engaged as they attempted to reach the gate to open it. Captain Lumsden was killed outright and Lieutenant Cooper severely wounded but Colonel Ewart fought on, accounting himself for six mutineers. Private Peter Grant, seizing a rebel's sword, came to the rescue of his hard-pressed Colonel and ran through a further five of his assailants. In the final struggle to open the gate it was rushed from the outside by the 4th Panjabis.

> 'Fortunately Sabahdar Mukarrab Khan, a Pathan from Bajaur, pushed his left arm, on which was a shield, between the heavy doors, preventing them from being closed. On his arm being badly wounded by a sword cut, he withdrew it, instantly thrusting in the other arm, when his right hand was all but severed from the wrist.' – Roberts.

With the gateway finally forced, the job of clearing the rebels out of the many small rooms and hiding places was undertaken. Then with the Sikandarbagh taken, they were faced with the necessity of taking the even larger and more formidable Shah Najaf. Sir Colin ordered the 93rd to be reformed and addressed them:

> 'Soldiers! I had no intention of employing you again today, but the Shah Najaf must be taken this evening. The artillery cannot drive the enemy out so you must with the bayonet, and I will lead you myself.'

H. Alison describes the action thus:

'Peel, manning all his guns, worked his pieces with redoubled energy, and under cover of the ironstorm, the 93rd, excited to the highest degree, with flashing eyes and nervous tread, rolled on in one vast wave. The grey-haired veteran of many fights rode, with his sword drawn, at their head. Keen was his eye as when, in the pride of youth, he led the stormers at St. Sebastian, his Staff crowded round him. Hope, too, with his towering form and gentle smile was there, leading, as ever was his wont, the men by whom he was loved so well. As they approached the nearest angle of the enclosure the

'The Storming of the Sikanderbagh by the 93rd Regiment, November 11, 1857'.    Orlando Norie.

soldiers began to drop fast, but without any check they reached its foot. There, however, they were brought to a stand.'

The struggle continued through the night and just after sunrise the following morning Sir Colin ordered the 93rd Regimental Colour to be uncased and displayed, with a feather bonnet on the tip of a pole, to signal to the Residency how far he had advanced. Lieutenant MacBean, Sergeant Hutchison and a twelve-year-old drummer-boy, Drummer Ross, scaled a minaret of the Shah Najaf to display the Colour, which was greeted by a burst of fire from the rebels. Undeterred, Ross waved his bonnet and defiantly played 'The Cock o' of the North'.

In the mopping-up operations which followed the breaching of the major defences, large numbers of the enemy were killed. The Residency was reached five days after the first attack and a further three days were spent in evacuating the personnel and baggage. By magnificent generalship Sir Colin Campbell managed to smuggle out 1,000 sick and wounded, 600 women and children, the family of the King of Oudh with treasure and baggage, and £250,000 of Government money as well as quantities of stores without exposing them to a single shot from the enemy. It was a remarkable feat in an altogether remarkable operation.

Later it was announced that seven Victoria Crosses had been awarded to men of the 93rd for individual acts of heroism.

The following month the 93rd were again involved in action, this time at the Battle of Cawnpore. Again the rebels were thoroughly routed with great loss of men and equipment. On December 7 the 93rd were withdrawn to Gwalior where they were able for the first time for twenty-seven nights to sleep without their accoutrements.

The 93rd were engaged in many desperate actions before the mutiny was finally quelled in 1859. They then remained

*Army Museums Ogilby Trust*

*Princess Louise's Argyll and Sutherland Highlanders at Aldershot in 1881.*

in India for a further ten years before returning to Scotland in 1870. They remained at home until 1879, when they were posted to Gibraltar for two years. On July 1, 1881 under a reorganization of the Army, as has already been related, the title of the regiment was changed to Princess Louise's Argyll and Sutherland Highlanders. Under this amalgamation with the 91st, the old Argyllshire Regiment became the 1st Battalion and the Sutherland Highlanders formed the 2nd Battalion.

# Chapter 5

## Princess Louise's Argyll and Sutherland Highlanders, 1881–1914

THE reorganization under which the 91st and the 93rd became amalgamated was known as the Cardwell system after its originator. This system which remained in force until 1948 was based on giving each newly-formed unit a territorial name and allocating to it a recruiting area. By this arrangement Sutherlandshire was allocated to the Seaforth Highlanders and Argyllshire was the only highland county given to the Argyll and Sutherland Highlanders. The other counties were Dumbarton, Renfrew, Stirling, Clackmannan and Kinross – areas from which they had previously had very few recruits. Thus it was inevitable that the regiment should lose much of its Highland traditions and become more and more Lowland in its composition attracting many English and Irish to its ranks.

The effect of the amalgamation was that the 1st and 2nd Battalions should be regarded as completely interchangeable, each supplying drafts for the other and with promotion running through the whole regiment, officers being posted from the one battalion to the other as vacancies occurred. It was inevitable that, with the different traditions of the two regiments, there should be some initial friction, but this was soon outgrown and a real *esprit de corps* established.

The Sutherland tartan (very similar to the Campbell) was adopted and the Regimental badge was specially designed by H.R.H. the Princess Louise. It is made up of the Campbell Boar's Head and the Sutherland Wild Cat linked together by the Princess's cyphers. On July 25, 1881, the depot companies of the old 93rd moved to Stirling Castle, which now became the depot for both battalions with the responsibility for supplying them with drafts.

The 1st Battalion remained in Cape Town until 1883, when they moved first to Natal and then, in the following year to Zululand, where the Zulu leaders were again proving disobedient. All that was required, as it turned out, was a show of strength to bring the rebel leaders into submission. There followed seven more years in foreign stations, three in Ceylon and four in Hong Kong before the regiment returned home.

They were serving in Dublin when, in the summer of 1899, the Commanding Officer received a confidential communication to say that the regiment would form part of an expeditionary force if the political situation in South Africa grew worse.

On October 25 they were inspected by Lord Roberts, V.C., who told the men

> 'that it gave him great pleasure to see them so fit and ready in all respects for active service.'

Two days later they embarked, 29 officers and 1,078 other ranks strong, for the South African war.

The battalion arrived at Cape Town on November 17 and was at once rushed up-country to reinforce Lord Methuen, whose severely depleted command was approaching the Modder River on its way to the relief of Kimberley. Lord Methuen, in spite of strong evidence to the contrary, was convinced that the Boers only held the line of the Modder with a few guns and snipers. As the 1st Battalion approached the bridge, however, they came under very heavy fire from the other side and were forced to lie down.

Thereinafter, and in spite of contradictory orders, they advanced by stages towards the river until about midday

Lieutenants Irvine and Baker-Carr of A Company found themselves with about 150 men a short distance from the river bank. Baker-Carr, who was subsequently wounded, describes the crossing:

> 'We then made a dash for the river and formed a hand-in-hand chain across. The river was rather more than waist-deep and a fair current. Irvine and I were first over and stopped on the far side to pull a few men up the bank and then made for the houses. We went through these and then formed up all the men of the regiment we could collect. We then proceeded in open order along the right bank of the river, through thick oak trees and scrub.'

The rest of the regiment followed A Company across, but the heavy Boer fire took its toll. As a result of poor administration they had had no food for thirty-six hours and suffered terribly from thirst. At the same time the backs of their legs were burned raw by the scorching sun. They were forced to withdraw with total casualties of 30 killed and 92 injured.

The following morning they went into the attack again, only to find that the Boers had slipped away in the night.

By the beginning of December, Lord Methuen, having received reinforcements, considered he was strong enough to complete the last stage of his advance to the relief of Kimberley. He was opposed by five to six thousand Boers, who occupied the 4,000-foot rock-bound kopje of Magersfontein Hill. Lord Methuen's plan was to bombard the position and then rush it with the bayonet.

When the time came for the Highland Brigade to advance, it experienced considerable difficulty in keeping direction because of the uneven nature of the country. Worse, it had been assumed that the Boers would occupy a position on the high ground. Instead they had entrenched themselves in a forward position at the foot of the kopje. The result was that the British stumbled on the enemy long before they were expecting them. Colour-Sergeant McInnes gives a dramatic description of what followed:

'Suddenly from the hillside in front of us a bright light flashed twice, followed by a couple of rifle shots. Immediately, on the level in front of us, a concealed trench opened a terrific fire. The front of the hill was lit up by the flashes of rifles as though someone had pressed a button and turned on a million electric lights. The brigade seemed to stagger under the awful fire, but yet held their ground, and did not break. The order was given to lie down, but in that close formation we were getting shot like sheep.

'I remember distinctly the 91st getting the order to move to the right, and we had started moving in that direction when several very contradictory orders rang out, some calling to "fix bayonet and charge" etc. Then, this seemed to me what happened – The Black Watch, who were in front, could stand it no longer, and were driven back on the Seaforths (Colonel Hughes-Hallett, the only unwounded Commanding Officer, had ordered them to swing out to the right) who likewise were driven back on top of the Argylls. Then several started to shout "retire" and the next minute the brigade had lost all shape and were converted into a dismayed mob, running to seek cover anywhere and getting shot by the score as they did so.

'Then it was that I witnessed one of the bravest deeds I ever saw, for suddenly there broke forth the strains of "The Campbells are Coming", and there was Jimmy MacKay, the corporal piper of the 91st, standing up fearlessly playing the regimental tune, facing the storm of bullets in a valiant attempt to stop the retirement becoming a rout. The pipers of the various regiments broke out playing almost immediately after, and there can be no doubt that this altered the aspect of the fight considerably.'

Although the Highland Brigade was rallied, they were in a critical predicament. Their Commanding Officer, Lieutenant-Colonel Goff, had been killed by the first salvo and within a short space of time almost every officer was either killed or wounded. It is to the utmost credit of the Highland Brigade that they continued to maintain their position, lying in the open at almost point-blank range from the finest shots in the world, from four in the morning until two in the afternoon. During the whole of this time they received no orders of any kind and were tortured by hunger and thirst. Their only support were British guns, without whose protective barrage almost the whole brigade would have been eliminated. As *The Times* reported: 'Rarely have troops gone through such an ordeal.'

Shortly after 2 p.m. the attack on Magersfontein was abandoned and Lord Methuen retreated to his original line on the Modder River. In February 1900 the Argylls were in action again at Koodoosberg, where they achieved their objective of containing the Boers. Then they were recalled to the Modder River by the Commander-in-Chief, Lord Roberts, who told them

> 'There is a lot of fighting to be done, and I mean the Highlanders to have their share of it. I have always had Highlanders with me; I do not mean to do without them now.'

It is a measure of the spirit of the Highland Brigade that the announcement was cheered to the echo.

The Commander-in-Chief was as good as his word. Within a few days the Highland Brigade was again in the thick of the fight, this time at Paardeberg Drift. This time the Argylls were ordered to advance on Kitchener's Kopje, marching forward four paces apart. General Colville records watching the advance with awe and wonder while there was nothing he could do to help the thin line as they marched across the open plain into a hail of lead.

> 'Thinner and thinner it grew, and thicker and thicker the brown patches on the grass behind it. What men were

able to do, the Highlanders did; but there seems to be a law which fixes the exact amount of thinning which a body of civilized men can stand. It has nothing to do with fear; a battalion will advance without a waver, under a storm of bullets, up to a certain point; on reaching that point it is possible that the enemy's fire may have slackened, but if the gaps are too big it will halt.'

This is what happened, the brigade came to a halt about 500 yards short of the enemy position. It was the culmination of two long marches in one day, five hours' sleep followed by fourteen hours under fire until night came. Yet the following morning they were ready to rejoin battle when it was heard that negotiations had been entered into over a surrender by Cronje. At the end of the battle of Paardeberg, the Argylls had seven officers left, the Black Watch six and the Seaforths five.

With reinforcements constantly arriving from Stirling, the regiment continued to be involved in action and, on July 15, 1900, were made part of Sir Ian Hamilton's flying column. The object was to sweep the country north of Pretoria where General Botha was being very active. It was a rigorous interlude often involving forced marches in appalling weather. During the 43 days of the operation, the battalion only had 5 days of rest, fought two actions and averaged over 12 miles a day.

The following year they formed part of Colonel Benson's column, which was one of the most effective forces harrying the Boers. *The Times* describes the operation thus:

'From the end of July onwards ... one only British column operated in the high veldt – namely, that under Colonel Benson. A few more operating as skilfully and energetically in the same district might well have thwarted Botha's plans (for the invasion of Natal). There was nothing new in Benson's methods, which may be described in two words as "night raiding". All British leaders had realised that the best way of catching a commando at a disadvantage was to march for it by night and attack at dawn. The Boer detested this method. Once in the saddle, rifle in hand, and a full bandolier buckled round him, he was more than a match for a British trooper; pounced on while still in laager, he was liable to panic. To carry out a good night raid several things were essential – a dashing leader, thoroughly efficient mounted troops and, above all, excellent local intelligence. Benson's intelligence officer was Colonel Wools-Sampson, who used trained native and Boer scouts. Benson's force was now a reliable weapon, and its colonel was a born guerilla leader. He and Sampson carried out a demoralising system of warfare.'

The Argylls could not possibly have kept up with Benson's mounted troops but for their magnificent marching whereby they gained the nickname of Benson's Horse.

The following year, 1902, the Argylls were made part of Kitchener's column at Klerksdorp, assembled to avenge Lord Methuen's disaster at Tweebosch. They started a continuous week of marching to reach Kleesdorp but the talk was of nothing but the prospects of peace, which was finally declared on June 1. 'At last, after two years and seven months of it, one can hardly believe it,' one officer wrote in his diary.

The 1st Battalion remained in South Africa for a year after the end of hostilities. They attended the Coronation Parade at Johannesburgh and, later in the year, the unveiling of the Highland Brigade Memorial by Lord Milner at Magersfontein. Then on May 6, 1903, they embarked for Southampton, later taking up quarters at Bordon. From 1905 to 1909 they were at Chatham and were honoured in 1908 by being selected to provide the King's Guard in London.

In 1909 they were posted to Malta and later moved to India, where they were stationed when the 1914 war broke out.

*Silver centre-piece of the Argylls, purchased to commemorate their part in the South African War.*

The 2nd Battalion were on home service from 1881 to 1891, during which time they also were honoured by being appointed to find guards and carry out other duties at Windsor Castle during the absence of the Scots Guards in Egypt.

On Christmas Day 1891 they arrived at Karachi, later travelling on to Ambala, where they were inspected by Lord Roberts, the Commander-in-Chief. There followed several years of routine duties during which the battalion acquitted itself well in manoeuvres and in inter-regimental sporting events.

In the summer of 1897 the regiment received orders to mobilize and join an expedition to the Tochi Valley, to avenge the treacherous murder of six British officers by the Waziris. Although the regiment did not in the end become involved in action in Waziristan, the journey proved most rigorous. Marching was by night on account of the extreme heat by day; but in spite of this, there were many casualties from heat apoplexy. With the onset of winter they suffered intense cold as well as several deaths from enteric fever and dysentery.

The regiment remained in India until 1907, during which period Lieutenant-General Sir A. Hunter remarked:

'Lieutenant-Colonel S. Paterson has, I think, a right to be proud to stand at the head of such a fine battalion as the 2nd Argyll and Sutherland Highlanders. The fighting efficiency of these Highlanders today justifies, and I believe establishes, their claim to be considered as the equals of even the best of their gallant predecessors in the glorious history of bygone days.'

In 1907 they proceeded to South Africa where they received a draft from home of 1 officer and 222 other ranks. This was extremely welcome, as recruitment was again presenting a considerable problem. Recruiting parties met with little success so that, before leaving India, a special bounty had been offered to serving soldiers who would be prepared to extend their period of service – an offer which was accepted by over 200 men.

The regiment returned home in the last days of 1909, after eighteen years' service abroad. Already there was a general awareness amongst many responsible people that a major conflict in Europe was inevitable and troops on home service were being rigorously trained in anticipation of it. Much of the 2nd Battalion's training was carried out at Stobs Camp near Hawick, but they also took part in the large exercises ordered by Scottish Command. They also found time for other activities. It is, for example, interesting to note that on Balaclava Day 1910, the battalion gave a dinner for 27 veterans of the Crimea and the Mutiny of whom no less than five had been at Balaclava in 1854.

*Officer of the Argyll and Sutherland Highlanders in review order, 1914.*

At the beginning of 1914 the 2nd Battalion decided to build a permanent memorial to their origins. It was decided to erect a cairn at Skail in Strathnaver, County of Sutherland. Most of the work was carried out by members of the battalion. A tablet was inscribed:

'To Commemorate the Place where the First Gathering of Men of the 93rd Sutherland Highlanders took place on the Formation of the Regiment in September, 1800.'
Erected by the Officers, N.C.O.'s and Men of the 2nd Battalion Argyll and Sutherland Highlanders.

The cairn was unveiled in the summer of 1914 although the work had not been entirely completed. The finishing touches had to be made by the local inhabitants as, before they could be carried out by members of the battalion, Great Britain was at war with Germany.

# *Chapter*
# 6

## *1914–1918*

B RITAIN declared war against Germany at 11 a.m. on
August 4, 1914. The 2nd Battalion of the Argyll and
Sutherland Highlanders received their mobilization
orders at 5.30 p.m. on the same day and, two days later,
were at full strength. They left Fort George on August 9
and arrived at Boulogne on the 14th, where they were given
an enthusiastic welcome by the local population – a welcome
which was made all the more warm because there was some
doubt amongst the French whether we would come so
rapidly to their aid.

The 2nd Battalion were part of the 19th Brigade of the
Expeditionary Force. Although they were in support at the
first Battle of Mons, their first heavy engagement came on
August 26 at the Battle of Le Cateau. At 11 a.m. they were
ordered forward to support the 14th Brigade. Halves of B
and C Companies reinforced the front line with the King's
Own Yorkshire Light Infantry and the Suffolks, who
occupied a salient overlooking Le Cateau. It was a difficult
position, being enfiladed by the enemy from the north and
both the 2nd Battalion and the Suffolks suffered heavy
casualties. Of this early action the British Official History
records:

'The Suffolks and the Argylls opened rapid fire to
their front with terrific effect. Two officers of the
Highlanders in particular bringing down man after man,
and counting their scores out loud as if in competition.
The Germans kept sounding the British "Cease Fire"
and gesticulating to persuade the men to surrender, but

A.S.H.—6

in vain. At length a rush of the enemy from the rear bore down all resistance, and the Suffolks and their Highland comrades were overwhelmed. They had for nine hours been under an incessant bombardment, which pitted the whole ground with craters, but they fought to the very last, covering themselves with glory.'

The collapse of this position was followed by a general retreat during which the situation became more and more confused. The various units of the 19th Brigade became so split up that regimental identities became lost. It was four or five days before the remnants of the regiment became reunited. Casualties were: Officers missing, 11, other ranks killed or wounded about 150, other ranks missing 300.

There followed the Battles of the Marne (Sept. 7th–10th) and the Battle of the Aisne (Sept. 12th–15th) before the position started to settle down. Just before the Aisne, the Argylls, who were in reserve, were passed by Sir John French who stopped and addressed them. He said:

'I have not before had an opportunity of seeing the 93rd and of thanking them for their work at Le Cateau. It was only by our troops holding on for so long, and I speak especially of the 93rd, that the French were saved from a very serious reverse. Please let your men know this.'

The Germans subsequently confirmed that the delay caused at Le Cateau was vital. The rifle fire of the British was so heavy that the Germans thought they had come up against a machine-gun battalion!

On October 21, the 19th Brigade were in action again, this time in the Battle of Armentières. Their first role was in support of the French dismounted cavalry but, as the situation crumbled, they were forced to take up a defensive position at La Boutillerie where they remained under constant attack and shell-fire for nine days. In the end a determined attack by the Germans reached the British lines and broke through the Middlesex position. The 93rd finally beat off the attack and sent a party to support the Middlesex. They drove the enemy out of their position at the point of the bayonet, killed 56 and took 94 prisoners.

The winter of 1914–15 found the 93rd in a particularly uncomfortable position. Major hostilities had perforce ceased because of the weather, which made troop movement impossible, but there was constant 'crater fighting'. The battalion occupied trenches which were lower than those of the enemy with the result that the water pumped out by the Germans found its way downhill so that our men were sometimes up to their waists and could get very little respite.

It was the summer of 1915 before the Allies made their

*Imperial War Museum*

*Men of the Argylls in the trenches during the winter of 1914–15.*

first major attack against the Germans – an attack which was led by the 19th Brigade at Loos. It was not a successful venture. In the first place it was decided to use gas, but not sufficient attention was paid to the wind. The result was that, when the main attack started at 6.30 a.m., the gas was still hanging around our own positions and even blowing back into the faces of our advancing troops. It had no effect on the Germans, who were prepared for the attack and had a considerable advantage over our men, who were encumbered with gas-masks.

No sooner had A Company moved than they lost every one of their officers and the other Companies fared little better. The two leading platoons actually reached the German front line, but their casualties were appalling. Only 11 men survived. By the time the abortive attack had been called off, the casualty list numbered 315, with nothing achieved.

At the end of 1915 the Argylls and the Middlesex were transferred to the 98th Brigade in the 33rd Division. There followed six months of sporadic trench warfare including intense mining, counter-mining and raiding in the area of the La Bassée Canal. On July 1, 1916, the British launched their great offensive on the River Somme. The 33rd Division moved into the battle on the 7th of July and were engaged in this desperate contest in various sectors until winter brought an end to hostilities.

During that time, they fought a series of defensive and offensive engagements, notably at Bazentin-le-Petit, High Wood and Les Boeufs, finally coming to rest at the end of the year at Bouchavesnes, where trench-foot was the chief enemy and was overcome by excellent administration.

The two main offensive actions were at High Wood on August 18, where numerous other regiments had suffered heavy losses and where the battalion also were unsuccessful and had heavy casualties. Bombarded by our own guns for two hours on the starting line, and with our plans for gas

73

and offensive mines failing, only part of B Company succeeded in penetrating the enemy's defences. They remained there for six hours until all ammunition was expended and then had to withdraw. On that day, 5 officers and 26 men were killed and the wounded and missing numbered 158.

At the end of August the battalion was successful at their second attempt in capturing the heavily defended

*Imperial War Museum*

*A machine-gun detachment of the 2nd Battalion, Argyll and Sutherland Highlanders 'at rest' during the second Battle of the Scarpe, April 1917.*

Pommières-Redoubt on the Pozières Ridge, while their last attack in the Somme Battle was carried out with great success on the Le Transloy Ridge, overlooking Les Boeufs. Here they captured an objective heaped with the dead of Units of three other British Divisons who had been beaten back by the enemy with heavy casualties in previous attacks. The Somme fighting cost them heavily as they lost a total of 25 officers and 650 other ranks between July and December.

In April 1917 there came the second Battle of the Scarpe, in which the 2nd Battalion played an heroic role. As part of a general attack to widen the breach already made in the Hindenburg Line, the Argylls, the Middlesex and the 4th Suffolks were given the task of forcing their way forward to meet up with the 100th Brigade, attacking from the south. The action began at 4.45 a.m. and by 6.30 a.m. Captain Henderson, commanding A Company was able to report that their objective had been attained. At 10 a.m., however, the Germans carried out a successful counter-attack, driving back the Suffolks. Thus the Argylls and 170 seventy of the Middlesex were isolated. Attacked from both front and rear, they held on tenaciously, Captain Henderson personally leading a bayonet charge against a large body of the enemy. By 7.30 of the following morning, patrols discovered the remnants of this gallant band had made themselves so unpleasant to the enemy that they had withdrawn.

Every survivor of the Argylls and the Middlesex was recommended for an award for bravery and Captain Henderson gained the posthumous award of the Victoria Cross.

The G.O.C. of 7th Corps wrote:

'The incident of the two companies (one of the 1st Middlesex and one of the Argyll and Sutherland Highlanders) being isolated for nearly twenty-four hours until relieved will no doubt live in the history of those distinguished Regiments . . .'

while General Allenby commanding the 3rd Army commented:

'I have read this account with great pride and admiration. I congratulate all ranks in the 2nd Battalion Argyll and Sutherland Highlanders and 1st Middlesex, on the staunchness and bravery of those two splendid Companies.'

In September came the third Battle of Ypres where the 93rd took part first in a difficult and highly successful operation at Polygon Wood during the long drawn-out battle of the Menin Road. This was followed by a short, well-earned rest in billets before another long and uncomfortable winter in the trenches at Passchendaele, where they relieved the Canadians on the day after its capture.

With the coming of spring, the position was indeed grave. The Germans started a series of terrific attacks along a fifty-mile front, designed to separate the British from the French, take the Channel Ports and destroy the British Army. Sir Douglas Haig, the Commander-in-Chief, issued his now famous Order of the Day:

'There is no other course open to us but to fight it out. Every position must be held to the last man; there must be no retirement. With our backs to the wall and believing in the justice of our cause, each one of us must fight on to the end. The safety of our homes, the freedom of mankind, depend alike upon the conduct of each one of us at this critical moment.'

The whole army responded in the most magnificent way in the desperate fighting which followed, and the 93rd more than played its part in repelling the German attacks in the Meteren area, where they helped to stop the wide-open gap made when the Portuguese army were driven back in disorder by the enemy in an unexpected offensive. By mid-summer the crisis had passed and, with America coming into the war, we were able to switch to an offensive role and assault the Hindenburg Line. The Argylls took part in several minor actions and were in the van of the pursuit of the enemy after the Battle of Cambrai up to the line of the Selle and on to the Forêt de Mormal. A week before the Armistice was declared they were taking part in the Battle of the Sambre and preparing for a further advance against the enemy. Thus for the battalion the final stages of the conflict were enacted close to Le Cateau, where they had had their first baptism of fire four long years before.

The fortunes of the 1st Battalion took a rather different course to that of the 2nd. At the outbreak of war they were stationed in India but they were soon under orders to return for service in France. They arrived in Le Havre as part of the 81st Brigade of the 27th Division just before Christmas Day. They were then moved up in support of the 80th Brigade for their first taste of the trenches. No fighting was possible because of the dreadful weather and the water-logged ground, which proved particularly unpleasant for the troops just arrived from India.

With the coming of April the weather improved and the battalion moved out of Ypres for another tour of trench duty. Little could they have guessed when they put on their boots on the morning of April 12 that it would be thirty-six hours before they took them off again. Information had been gained from a prisoner that the Germans were about to launch a large-scale attack on the 15th and that they would use poison gas. When the date came and went without an attack, it was assumed that the information was incorrect. In fact, the attack had simply been postponed because of unfavourable wind.

When it was launched a week later it had the advantage of surprise. Although the 27th Division was not immediately involved, the French troops to the immediate north gave way and the situation became critical. A withdrawal was ordered to Sanctuary Wood to protect the divisional flank. Then, on May 8, the division was subjected to a terrific bombardment in their new position, which was the prelude to a determined attack. The crisis of the second Battle of Ypres had been reached.

For five days fortunes swayed to and fro. The enemy, supported by their greatly superior artillery, attacked continually and were as often counter-attacked. The front line trenches of the Allies were so heavily shelled that they were virtually useless to either side and became part of No Man's Land. At one stage the situation was only saved by a courageous advance by B and C Companies of the Argylls, who moved forward in perfect formation across the shell-swept country to support the crumbling line.

By May 13 the enemy force was spent and the bombard-

*Imperial War Museum*

*Argyll and Sutherland Highlanders returning to their billets, May 1917.*

ment ceased. Two days later the battalion was relieved and they retired to a bivouac area behind the lines. Shortly after their arrival they were visited by Field-Marshal Sir John French, who addressed the brigade in the following words which, better than anything, describes the importance of the battle in which the 1st Battalion had played such an honourable part.

'I came over to say a few words to you and to tell you how much I, as Commander-in-Chief of this Army, appreciate the splendid work you have all done during the recent fighting. You have fought the second Battle of Ypres, which will rank amongst the most desperate and hardest fights of the war. You may have thought because you were not attacking the enemy that you were not helping to shorten the war. On the contrary, by your splendid endurance and bravery, you have done a great deal to shorten it. In this, the second Battle of Ypres, the Germans tried by every means in their power to get possession of that unfortunate town. They concentrated large forces of troops and artillery and, further than that, they had recourse to that mean and dastardly practice, hitherto unheard of in civilized warfare, namely the use of asphyxiating gases.

'You have performed the most difficult, arduous and terrific task of withstanding a stupendous bombardment by heavy artillery, probably the fiercest artillery fire ever directed against troops, and warded off the enemy's attacks with magnificent bravery. By your steadiness and devotion both the Germans' plans were frustrated. He was unable to get possession of Ypres – if he had done this he would probably have prevented neutral powers from intervening, and he was unable to distract us from delivering our attack, in conjunction with the French in Arras-Armentières district. Had you failed to repulse his attacks and made it necessary for more troops to be sent to your assistance, our operations in the south might not have been able to take place, and would certainly not have been as successful as they have been.

'Your Colours have many famous names emblazon-
ed on them, but none will be more famous, or more well
deserved, than that of the Second Battle of Ypres. I
want you, one and all, to understand how thoroughly I
realise and appreciate that you have done. I wish to
thank you, each officer, non-commissioned officer and
man, for the services you have rendered by doing your
duty so magnificently and I am sure that your country
will thank you too.'

The second Battle of Ypres was the only engagement of
note in which the 1st Battalion took part in France. Shortly
after the battle they were moved to Armentières where they
were played into the town by the pipe-band of the 2nd
Battalion. When they relieved the sector of the trenches held

*Imperial War Museum*

*A patrol crossing a damaged railway bridge, France 1918.*

by the Buffs they found that the 2nd Battalion was holding the line immediately on their right. This was the first time the two regular battalions had found themselves side by side in war.

Summer passed with little incident and most of the autumn was spent in billets before entraining for Marseilles, where they embarked on November 28, for Salonika.

The object of sending the 27th Division to Salonika was to support our ally Serbia, who was being attacked by the Bulgarians and Austrians, while Rumania and Greece remained ostensibly neutral. By the time the division had reached Salonika, however, Serbia had already been lost. Instead of advancing into that country they occupied a line in Macedonia about 50 miles inside the Greek frontier. Although they were invited into Greece on the personal responsibility of the Greek Prime Minister, there was no doubt that the people were pro-German, which made the role of the Allies a difficult one.

Although after their experiences in the water-logged trenches of France, the move to Salonika must at first have seemed an improvement in their lot, it was not long before the men of the division realized that they were not to occupy a bed of roses. The climate varied between the extreme heat of the period from March to October and the cold and wet of the rest of the year.

The hot summers were made the more trying because the countryside offered little shade and the irritating Balkan dust got into everything from eyes to food. The bad climatic conditions brought on attacks of malaria and dysentery, from which the troops suffered severely. At the same time, the work of building fortifications and a heavy training programme under constant fear of an attack put a serious strain on the general morale.

After a few months outside Salonika, the battalion moved to take up a position on the south side of the Struma valley. They occupied high ground overlooking a plain twelve miles wide through which ran the River Struma, which was an obstacle 100 yards wide. Here the construction of defences was recommenced, while the malaria epidemic became ever more virulent.

It probably came as something of a relief when it was learned that the monotony was to be broken by an attack which had as its object the establishment of a bridgehead over the river. The plan behind this limited offensive was to hold the Bulgarian troops on the Struma front during the Franco-Serbian operations at Monastir.

The attack on the first objective – the village of Bala – was carried out on September 30 and proved completely successful. The task of the 1st Battalion of the Argylls was to pass through the new position and carry the second objective which was the village of Zir. This proved a much more difficult task. Once the enemy had recovered from their initial surprise they put up a most stubborn defence. However, by seven o'clock in the evening both objectives had been attained and held in spite of several determined counter-attacks. It proved expensive. Casualties were 2 officers killed and 12 wounded; 20 other ranks killed and 87 wounded. A high price to pay for a comparatively meagre result.

There followed another period north of the Struma River building breastworks, digging trenches, wiring and construction of dug-outs to complete the winter defence line. At the same time a constant exploration of the enemy's position by patrols was carried on, which occupied them during the wet winter months. Then, with the advent of the hot weather, it was decided to withdraw from the malaria-ridden Struma plain and retire to the hills some six miles distant.

In spite of this precaution the chief enemy continued to be malaria. Quinine was compulsory and mosquito nets issued, but the official statistics still showed that over 80 per cent of the army had become infected. From August to

October the battalion showed hospital admissions at the rate of 106 per month, while discharges were only 35.

The beginning of 1918 brought a change for the better for our troops. The Greeks finally decided to join the Allies and they were handed over the Struma front while the 27th Division moved to Vardar to the west, where they took over from the French. There followed a period of active and effective patrol work against the Bulgars, which finally resulted in the battalion establishing a firm supremacy of No Man's Land on its own front. The object was to contain the enemy while efforts were made by the Serbians and the French to penetrate the enemy front line on the left and threaten his communications.

This proved successful and on September 16 it was heard that the Serbians were pouring through a breach and that the Bulgarian army was in full retreat. On September 30 at 6 a.m. the cessation of hostilities was announced.

A few days later the Army Council telegraphed the Commander-in-Chief:

> 'The War Cabinet wish me to convey to you and to all ranks under your command their heartiest congratulations on the decisive success which has at last crowned the operations of the British Forces in Macedonia. In common with their Allied comrades they have for three years cheerfully sustained the burden of an arduous campaign in an unhealthy climate, without the stimulus of great offensive operations and few opportunities for leave. The endurance and devotion of the troops have now secured results, which will profoundly influence the course of war in favour of the Allied cause.'

Although the war was to continue in France for another six weeks, both sides recognized that the fall of Bulgaria marked the beginning of the end. General Ludendorff put it in its correct perspective when he wrote about the great Allied offensive of 1918:

'August 8th was the blackest day for the German Army in the history of this war. This was the worst experience I had to go through except for the events that, from September 15 onwards, took place on the Bulgarian front and sealed the fate of the quadruple Alliance.'

By the time hostilities were over the 1st Battalion was sadly reduced in numbers. Malaria and influenza had reduced the ration strength to a mere 237 of whom more than 100 were employed on Transport or Quartermaster duties behind the line. No company exceeded 45 in number and all were organized on a two-platoon basis. In spite of their depleted ranks, however, they continued to perform guard and other duties until they finally embarked for England in May 1919.

It is not possible in this short history to give the details of the activities of any but the two regular battalions during the Great War. Some idea of the total contribution made by the Argyll and Sutherland Highlanders may be gained from the Scottish Great War Memorial erected at Edinburgh Castle.

The dedication reads:

'Ne Obliviscaris'
To the Memory of
431 Officers and 6,475 Other Ranks
of the Regiment
Who Gave Their Lives
For King and Country
1914–1918

Regulars:
1st Battalion
91st (Argyllshire) Highlanders
2nd Battalion
93rd (Sutherland) Highlanders
Special Reserve
3rd and 4th Battalions

Territorials
5th (Renfrewshire)
6th (Renfrewshire)
7th (Stirlingshire)
8th (Argyllshire)
9th (Dumbartonshire)

Service Battalions
10th, 11th, 12th, 13th, 14th, 15th

'Mons'                          'Somme, 1916, '18.'
'Le Cateau'                     'Arras, 1917, '18.'
'Marne, 1914–18.'               'Cambrai, 1917, '18.'
'Ypres, 1915, '17, '18.'        'Doiran, 1917, '18.'
'Loos.'                         'Gaza.'

Sans Peur
Princess Louise's
Argyll and Sutherland Highlanders

# Chapter
# 7

## 1919 – 1939

FOLLOWING the signing of the Armistice, arrangements began at once for the 1st Battalion to complete its foreign service tour which had been interrupted by the war. They were assembled in Glasgow, where the final peace celebrations took place on the anniversary of the declaration of war and, after a number of false alarms, embarked at full strength for India on October 24. At Port Said they heard that their station which had originally been Bangalore had been changed to Poona.

The India to which they returned was a very different one from the country they had left in 1914. There was an increasing feeling of unrest amongst the population and the more vociferous elements were clamouring for the removal of the British. Much of the glamour, too, had departed. In place of the colourful uniforms and ceremonial parades were drab khaki and military exercises. The role of the battalion was to quell industrial unrest, but although the threat was ever-present, there was little actual action. Much time was spent in performing the routine duties of barrack life and the opportunity taken to train the high proportion of young soldiers who had replaced the war veterans.

The Indian interlude lasted four years. Then, at the beginning of 1924 they sailed for their new station, which was to be Egypt. There they settled down at Ismailia and resumed the usual round of parades and inter-battalion sporting events at which, incidentally, they excelled. Then, quite suddenly, in August, they were moved to Khartoum in the

Sudan, where political unrest and demonstrations were moving towards a point of crisis.

It was not until November that the expected mutiny broke out. It was brought about by the assassination of Sir Lee Stack, the Governor-General of the Sudan, in Cairo. As a result the Egyptian troops were ordered to leave the Sudan and the British Garrison was given the task of receiving their surrender. The Egyptian troops in Khartoum adopted a policy of passive resistance until the impasse was broken by the open revolt of the Sudanese.

A running fight followed until finally the hard core of the mutineers was pinned down in the Egyptian Officers' Mess, where they had taken refuge. This strongly fortified building proved a tough nut to crack. The defenders were largely made of up instructors from the Egyptian Army Military School and were determined men as well as crack shots. It was only after two assaults had been repulsed that the position was finally carried. It was followed by mopping-up operations but when orders were given to surround the Egyptian Barracks, it was found that the mutineers had quietly disappeared into the desert. The mutiny was over.

There followed some further unrest in various out-stations but by the end of the year order had been restored and the battalion returned to Cairo, where they remained until 1928, when they returned to England. They had completed eighteen years' foreign service, broken by the war, which had also been fought far from home.

Two years before their departure from Cairo, it was decided that the Colours which had been presented to them by the Princess Louise in 1892 were too frail to outlast their tour of duty abroad. The silk had become so perished that it was impossible to emblazon on it the Battle Honours won in the Great War. The ceremony to present new Colours was undertaken by the High Commissioner, Lord Lloyd of Dolobran. Replying to the High Commissioner's speech of presentation, Lieutenant-Colonel G. W. Muir ended his expression of thanks with these appropriate words:

'We shall uphold the great traditions of the Regiment, to which we are so proud to belong, as our predecessors upheld them in the past.

Loyalty to our King,
Devotion to our Country
and
Pride in our Regiment.'

It was a promise which was to be well kept.

There followed a period of home service which was to last almost until the outbreak of the Second World War. Their first station was Shorncliffe, where they were visited by their Colonel-in-Chief, H.R.H. Princess Louise, who spent three days meeting the officers and men and their families. In the following year, 1930, they moved to Edinburgh, which was memorable as the first time the battalion had been stationed in its home country for thirty-two years. Not unnaturally their stay in Scotland was characterized by the number of calls made on them for ceremonial occasions, notably furnishing Royal guards both at Holyrood and Balmoral.

Training, however, was not neglected. The army was going through a great period of reorganization and re-thinking of its role, brought about by mechanization. During their time in Scotland, the 1st Battalion won the Machine Gun Cup, which may have been the reason why, when they were later posted to Tidworth, they were selected for the role of a mechanized machine-gun unit. They became part of an Experimental Brigade, trying out new tactics with mechanical transport and fighting vehicles, the results of which were to form the basis of the Army's new doctrine for the use of mechanized units.

As the prospect of another European war grew increasingly certain, they moved to Aldershot, where they took part for the first time in the Tattoo, but were also engaged in digging slit trenches on the once-sacred playing fields. Finally, in April 1939, they embarked once more for foreign parts. This time it was a short-term period in Palestine to take part in the quelling of the Arab rebellion.

By the time the regiment arrived in Palestine the back of the Arab rebellion had been broken. Their role, therefore, was largely that of policemen concerned with the mopping-up of stragglers from broken gangs and patrolling the area to prevent their reassembly. They carried out their task as the rumours of war in Europe became ever more persistent. When it finally broke out on September 3 it brought no change of role but a greatly increased anxiety amongst all ranks for the safety of those at home. History had repeated itself in that the coming of the Second World War again found them far from home with little likelihood of their immediate involvement. They formed part of the 2nd Middle East Reserve Brigade Group and it was difficult to see what active role they could play unless Italy came into the war, which she had not yet done.

The war did, however, bring about a resumption of activity by the rebels, who no doubt felt that our vigilance would be relaxed in our preoccupation with other matters. Several lively operations ensued, which resulted in the total destruction of the gangs which had again started to terrorize the local population.

In the midst of these activities the sad news arrived that their much-loved Colonel-in-Chief, H.R.H. Princess Louise, had died. She had been intimately associated with the regiment for almost seventy years, during which time her interest in its welfare had never flagged. She was repaid with the very real devotion of all ranks and their wives. Their pride in bearing her name was very sincere, and her death caused deep sadness.

The battalion now started on a course of rigorous training

against the day when they would be called upon to play an important part in the coming conflict.

The end of the Great War had found the 2nd Battalion greatly decreased in numbers. They were given a civic reception on their return to Stirling and then sent on leave pending the re-formation of the battalion. The 2nd, who had returned on a leave from France took over the 3rd Reserve Battalion who were stationed in Edinburgh and then joined the 1st Battalion for a short spell in Glasgow, where they were employed in combating the railway strike. Then, in 1920, they were sent to Ireland to help cope with the Sinn Fein Rebellion. It was not a particularly happy period, engaged as they were in the searching of houses and taking part in sweeps against the rebels. At the end of the year, following the brutal murder of fourteen British officers, they were given orders to arrest all officers of the Irish Republican Army. Within a few weeks they had captured about fifty.

On July 11, 1921 a cessation of hostilities was ordered. Shortly afterwards the battalion returned to Aldershot for a year before being sent to the Isle of Wight. They stayed there until 1927 when, after being presented with new Colours by H.R.H. Princess Louise, they sailed for the West Indies little short of a hundred years after the old 93rd Sutherland Highlanders had served there.

Life for the 2nd Battalion now became somewhat nomadic. Shortly after their arrival in the West Indies, they were posted to North China, gaining the odd distinction of being the only British regiment ever to be transported through the Panama Canal. Soon after they were again on the move, this time to Hong Kong, where they won the Machine Gun Cup at the Area Rifle meeting. They had a short emergency spell in Shanghai where they formed part of the International Force which guarded the Settlement during the Sino-Japanese War. This was followed by another spell in

Hong Kong when they again returned to Shanghai. During their time in China most of their energies were devoted to providing guards against Chinese pirates on ships plying up and down the Yangtse.

The regiment moved to Rawalpindi in India in 1933 with Jhelum as a centre, where they learned mountain warfare. They soon had an opportunity of practising this new type of activity, being engaged in both the Mohmand operations and the campaign in North Waziristan. For the former they had the distinction of being awarded what proved to be the last issue of the India General Service Medal and in the latter earned the first clasp of the new Service Medal.

With the troubles on the frontier settled, the battalion moved to Secunderabad in southern India, where, in order to bring them into line with the 1st Battalion, they found themselves being converted to a mechanized machine-gun unit. This move had hardly been completed before the orders were countermanded and they were reconverted to a Rifle Battalion.

During their stay in India the record of their football team deserves special note. In spite of being engaged in two frontier wars and in spite of the considerable turnover through time-expired men, they won the Northern Command cup in 1934 and 1935, and were runners-up, after extra time, in 1936. In 1937 they won the Muree Brewery Cup and the Durand Cup, which was the most important competition in India. In 1938 they won the Secunderabad Area Cup and were finalists in the Rovers' Cup in Bombay.

In August 1939 the battalion joined the 12th (Indian) Infantry Brigade and in this role were sent to Malaya. Within a few weeks of their arrival, war had broken out in Europe.

# *Chapter*
# 8

## *1939–1945*

IT was an anxious time for the 1st Battalion, who were engaged in routine security duties in Palestine in the first months of 1940, when it must have appeared to them that the whole of the Western Defences against Germany were crumbling. News that the evacuation at Dunkirk had been successfully accomplished was received with relief and when shortly afterwards, on June 10, it was learned that Italy had declared war, it was realized with satisfaction that it would not be long before the battalion was called upon to play an active role.

Two months later they were in the Western Desert and immediately occupied with preparing defences against the expected Italian advance into Egypt, which took place five days after their arrival.

Surprisingly the Italians, having successfully captured Sidi Barrani, seemed disinclined to press home their advantage. Thus a breathing space was vouchsafed to the battalion, during which they could acquire much needed training in the new skills called for by desert warfare. Many exercises were carried out so that when a further exercise was announced at the beginning of December, nothing very much was thought about it. It was only after the exercise started that it became known that this was to be the real thing and that an attack on the Italian position was planned.

It was in many ways a desperate undertaking, entailing an approach march of ninety miles over open desert against an enemy who were not only superior in numbers and occupying strongly defended positions but who had the advantage of a four-to-one air superiority. To have any chance of success, surprise had to be achieved and this must have seemed almost impossible in the circumstances.

When security was finally broken and the plan made known to our troops a special Order of the Day was issued by General Sir Archibald Wavell which was read to all ranks. It said:

> 'The result of the fighting in the Western Desert will be one of the decisive events of the war.
> 'The crushing defeat of the Italian forces will have an incalculable effect not only upon the whole position in the Middle East, not only upon the military situation everywhere, but on the future freedom and civilization throughout the world. It may shorten the war by very many months. It must be the firm determination of every man to do everything that in him lies, without thought of self, to win this decisive victory . . .'

In only one respect were the Allies superior to the enemy and that was in morale, and this proved to be the decisive factor. Incredibly, the approach march was completed without alarming the Italians unduly, who seemed to have thought it was just another exercise until it was too late. The Allied Force consisted of two divisions and they were opposed by four Italian corps. The 1st Argylls were in the van of the attack, leading and navigating for their Brigade and took the brunt of the enemy fire on the approach to Sidi Barrani, where they suffered heavy casualties.

They were completely successful, however, in achieving their allotted objective, where they harboured for the night after thirty-six hours without rations. By five o'clock the following morning they were on the move again, when it became apparent that the enemy had had enough. They could be seen retiring from all their positions while many thousands surrendered. In fact, the number of prisoners taken was an embarrassment to our troops until it was

*Imperial War Museum*

*A private of the 1st Battalion in the Mareth area, August 1940.*

discovered that they were so broken in morale that two or three soldiers were sufficient to guard a thousand Italians.

The taking of Sidi Barrani was not only one of the most skilful manoeuvres in British military history but had the added importance of being one of the first Allied successes in a war which had started disastrously for our cause.

There followed for the 1st Battalion a period devoted to guarding airfields and other places of strategic importance until, quite suddenly, whilst their C.O., Colonel Anderson, was on leave in Alexandria, they were ordered to leave for Amriya, in preparation for departure for an unknown destination. The unlucky Colonel Anderson and other members of the regiment, on their first night of leave, were awakened at 3 a.m. and ordered to proceed independently to Amriya. Thus started the adventure into Crete which was to prove so costly.

In the haste of the departure of the battalion it was only possible to load ten days' stores instead of the thirty days which was intended. Further complications ensued on landing in Crete, where the breakdown of the gear for lowering the landing craft caused further delays, which resulted in large quantities of petrol being left aboard. It was thus a very under-equipped force which landed on the south side of the island with orders to link up with the 14th Brigade, who were on the north coast at Heraklion.

A German attack on the island was imminent and, on the day following the landing, it became an actuality. Troops were poured into the island by parachute and a force of some 1,200 planes were committed to their support while there was no Allied air support whatsoever.

Under these conditions it is not surprising that matters should go ill. Repeated attempts were made to reach Heraklion by leap-frogging up the road, but the opposition proved too heavy. Eventually it was decided to use the mountain tracks and in this way part of the battalion got through. The situation, however, continued to deteriorate and three days later orders were received to evacuate Crete.

At this time the battalion was cut in two with the forward Companies in Heraklion and Headquarters, under the Second-in-Command, still held up at Ay Deka and out of communication. Messages sent by guides failed to reach them and eventually they were left behind and became prisoners of war. The remainder were taken off and brought back to Alexandria under heavy bombardment, which caused further casualties. Of the 655 who embarked on May 18, only 312 disembarked eleven days later. The 1st Battalion had become completely crippled.

The immediate result of this disaster was that when the 16th Brigade was sent to take part in the Syrian campaign, the Argylls were left behind on garrison duties in Khartoum, Cairo and Alexandria, being considered too weak to accompany them. It was a bitter disappointment. For the next two and a half years the crippled battalion was to pursue its lonely way through a wide area of the Middle East until they were finally brigaded again in February 1944. They served in Eritrea, arrived in Abyssinia in time to take part in the

*Imperial War Museum*

*Men of the 1st Battalion as part of 'No. 33 Beach Brick' during the landings in Sicily in 1944.*

capture of Gondar, the last Italian stronghold, and carried out internal security duties in the Sudan. Finally, after periods in the Western Desert, where they were in support at the Battle of Alamein, and Palestine, they were selected to play a crucial part in the invasion of Sicily.

For the purpose of the invasion the battalion temporarily lost its identity and became transformed into 'No. 33 Beach Brick', an organization specially formed to provide the labour and protection necessary to establish a Beach Area. For this purpose all manner of ancillary units became attached, with the result that the overall strength rose to 125 officers and 2,500 other ranks. In this unaccustomed role they stage-managed both the big Allied landing in Sicily and, two months later, the landing on the toe of Italy. In between these two operations they found themselves temporarily reconverted to a fighting unit holding a forward position – as their official historian records of the battalion

> 'sitting on hot, shadeless hills, very restricted as to move-
> ment, and desperately trying to remember its tactical
> training.'

In spite of the valuable services provided by the battalion over this long period, it must have come as welcome news all ranks that they were once again to become a combatant unit – this time as part of the 19th (Indian) Infantry Brigade of the 8th (Indian) Division, whom they joined in Italy in the mountainous country north of the River Sangro.

The first task for the battalion could hardly have been a more onerous one – none other than the crossing of the Rapido River at Cassino while leading the attack of the 8th Army. With typical Teutonic thoroughness, the Germans had erected formidable defences to add to the natural strength of their position: none the less, the crossing was made with heavy losses and a bridgehead established on the other side of the river, where the battalion was pinned down for a whole day under heavy fire, to which they were unable to reply. The expected tank support did not materialize, so at nightfall they withdrew.

At first light the following morning they again recrossed with tank support and carried the objectives allotted to them. It had, however, been a harrowing battle.

Following the storming of the famous monastery at Cassino by the Poles, it became essential to maintain the momentum of the advance and harrass the retreating enemy. In this the battalion played a prominent part, fighting many small actions in the drive to the River Arno. In three months the Eighth Army swept forward 220 miles to a position where they were ready to assault the formidable Gothic Line.

There followed a series of hard-fought actions. The Argylls were in the forefront of the battle at Monte Abetino, Monte Cavallera, Monte Cerere and the crossing of the River Senio leading up to the surrender of the German Army in Italy on May 2. A month later Brigadier Dobree bid farewell to the 19th Brigade and referred to the part played by the 1st Argylls in the following terms:

> 'The 1st Argyll and Sutherland Highlanders have lived up to the great traditions of their famous regiment. They have gone from strength to strength in the face of all opposition and won a reputation for dash and tenacity which cannot be excelled.'

The 1st Battalion had been abroad for six years and at the end of that time, despite casualties, it is worth recording that they were still, at the end of the war 99 per cent Scots.

The history of the 2nd Battalion during the last war is as different from its sister battalion as it is possible to imagine. The outbreak of war found them newly arrived in Malaya and training in country of which they had had no experience.

Much of Malaya is made up of either dense jungle or rubber plantations which give rather the same visibility as an English oak wood. It had long been the belief of the British tactical planners that the jungle formed an impassable barrier to the movement of troops. For this reason Singapore was considered impregnable from the north and the defences sited accordingly. It was certainly true that the jungle was impenetrable to untrained troops who would soon lose their direction and get lost. A trained man, however, could make steady progress through the densest undergrowth at the rate of about 1,000 yards an hour.

The Argylls formed part of the 12th Indian Infantry Brigade and it was fortunate that neither the Brigade Commander nor the Battalion Commander, Lieutenant-Colonel Stewart (or Achnacone – an Argyllshire man) accepted the previously held dogmas about jungle fighting.

*Imperial War Museum*

*The ill-fated 2nd Battalion training in Malaya in 1941.*

They had a year's grace from the time of their arrival until they were to be thrown into battle and they used it to work out completely new tactics which accepted not only that the jungle was possible battle terrain but that it could be the perfect medium for attack; offering, as it does, a completely covered approach.

The training was rigorous and sustained so that, in spite of a tendency by higher command to annex fully-trained jungle fighters for base duties and send untrained reinforcements, the battalion was in a high state of readiness when on December 8, 1941 it was heard that the Japs had landed on the north-east corner of Malaya. The 2nd Battalion, which was at Port Dickson, was at once entrained to Jerantut to be held in readiness to operate on whatever front the Japs decided to develop.

The situation was a desperate one. Within a few days of the outbreak of the war both the *Prince of Wales* and the *Repulse* were sunk, losing us command of the sea. In the air, although the Allies had well-sited aerodromes on the Malay Peninsula, the Japanese at once gained complete supremacy so that there was scarcely ever an Allied plane in the sky. Finally, the Japanese had a considerable weight of armour whilst the British had only a few armoured cars.

Contact was first made with the enemy at Titi-Karangan south of the Muda River. Orders were to deny a particular line to the enemy until a particular time, which was to be the pattern of things to come. For the first time the Argylls were to encounter the jungle tactics of the highly-trained Japanese. They fought on a set plan, which was to pin down the troops in front while sending encircling forces round both ends of the position, thus hoping to cut off the opposing force from their communications and so destroy them at their leisure. It was a manoeuvre which they employed time and time again, and one which the Argylls in particular became extremely adept at countering. It had long been impressed on them that the whole secret of jungle

*Imperial War Museum*

*A rare photograph of the 2nd Battalion in Malaya, 1941. All the men of the battalion were either lost or captured during the withdrawal to and eventual fall of Singapore.*

fighting was to hold on desperately to the initiative and to move fast. To do otherwise was to invite disaster in country where everything favoured the attacker.

The Argylls were allotted the role of covering the British withdrawal from the Thai frontier. Thus they were almost continuously involved in a series of battles designed to delay the Japanese advance and to inflict as many casualties as possible. It was found that the tactics in which they had been trained almost exactly matched those of the jungle-trained Japanese. Thus it became a battle of both wits and courage as they gave ground inch by inch on the long road back in face of an enemy vastly superior in numbers and fire-power.

Finally, after almost a month of dogged withdrawal they found themselves on the line of the Slim River and it was here, virtually the last possible defensive position before Kuala Lumpur, that Higher Command decided to make a stand. The battalion arrived there on January 4 under orders not to give up the position until the night of the 7th–8th. It was the first even semi-prepared defensive position in the experience of the battalion. Here they were reinforced with the draft of a hundred men from Singapore under Captain Drummond Hay. He had had considerable trouble with his draft because, when it was known that he was leaving to rejoin the battalion, every Argyll at the base employed on staff jobs whom Drummond Hay had been forbidden to take with him, paraded with the draft, demanding to be allowed to join.

The reinforcements arrived two hours before the Japanese main attack started on the early morning of January 7. It started with heavy mortar fire, followed by an attack by thirty or forty tanks against which there were no adequate defensive weapons; a road bridge demolition which had been prepared failed to go off, tank obstacles were pushed aside and a deep penetration made into our position. The Japanese commanded the road for a depth of about sixteen miles, causing the utmost confusion. With the British communications broken, resistance became a matter of isolated pockets holding out as best they could.

The Japanese swarmed everywhere, over-running our positions and cutting off parties of defenders. Survivors were able to tell of many acts of bravery but there must have been many more which went unrecorded because there was none left to tell the tale. By 6.30 p.m. the Battle of the River Slim was over. There were left only 3 officers and 90 other ranks of the battalion to be withdrawn to Singapore. Left behind in the jungle were many dead and small parties of survivors who had been over-run and were now trying to struggle back through the enemy to regain the battalion. Brigadier Stewart in his book on the campaign relates:

'The story of the numerous Argyll parties is too complex to be told here in detail. Starving, fever-ridden and exhausted, they struggled on, refusing to surrender. Lieutenant-Colonel Robertson (who had succeeded Brig. Stewart as C.O.) led the party of gradually dwindling strength until six weeks later, and 150 miles to the southward, reduced to a mere six, they ran into an ambush near Labis and all were killed. His batman, Private Bennett . . . has told of his leadership and care of his men and above all of his continually expressed determination never to surrender.

'Other parties, like those of Captain Lapsley and Captain Turner, also followed for the same distance behind the Jap advance, seeking a way through, and were still there when Singapore fell. Others again, amongst them Captain Bardwell, Lieutenant Montgomery Campbell, Platoon Sergeant-Major Colvin, Captain Broadhurst, the police officer, Sergeant Gibson, Lance-Corporal Grey and Corporal Robertson, made their way to the coast, got fishing boats, and sailed the 150 miles to Sumatra to join the Dutch. Captain Bardwell indeed, induced the Dutch to fly him back to Singapore, where he quickly got married and then rejoined the regiment in the battle.

'In their difficulties they met with great kindness from Chinese, Malays and Indians. To two of them, Private Stewart and Private Bennett (already mentioned as the C.O.'s batman) belongs the honour of remaining uncaptured for the next four years until liberation came. For most of this time they were with the

Chinese guerrillas, to whom they acted as weapon-training instructors. The regiment will be proud indeed of their initiative, skill and determination thus shown by its private soldiers.'

The withdrawal of the main body of survivors to Singapore was not without incident. Notably that, unlike their experience at the Battle of the Slim River, where a charge laid by the Sappers had failed to explode, on this occasion the charge exploded too soon, trapping part of our force on the wrong side of the bridge. Later two officers of the Argylls had to adopt the role of Sappers when another vital bridge had to be blown, but there were no R.E. personnel to do the job.

The spirit of the battalion may be judged by the fact that, all the way back down the road, in spite of being utterly exhausted, they continually salvaged abandoned vehicles so that, although their numbers were pathetically small, when they arrived at Singapore, their transport was over-strength.

Reorganization was begun immediately. Every Argyll who could hobble out of hospital and every member of the regiment in a staff job was collected. Soon the muster was 250. By dint of using Chinese volunteers as stretcher bearers it was possible to form two rifle companies and a small Headquarters Company. Then, at the end of January, they were joined by 200 Royal Marines who had survived the sinking of the *Prince of Wales* and the *Repulse*. This quickly earned them the nickname of the Plymouth Argylls, but they had every reason to be proud of their new comrades. By the end of January the battalion was 450 strong and ready to resume its proud role as the rearguard of the withdrawal. Thus began another desperate adventure.

If the Japanese had pressed home their advantage there would have been few indeed left amongst the party of Argylls who now returned to the mainland along the three-quarter mile causeway. In fact, the enemy were inexplicably slow in following up, so that the withdrawal went completely to plan and was achieved without any casualties. Even so the Argylls, last to leave the mainland, set an example in morale which made a deep impression on all who witnessed it. With the Japanese hard on their heels and the Sappers impatiently waiting to blow the causeway, they marched back in unhurried open order, their two remaining pipers playing 'A Hundred Pipers' and 'Hielan' Laddie'. Last of all came Drummer Hardy, almost alone on the long, open causeway. Exhorted to hurry, he maintained his own steady pace, too proud to show any haste as the sun rose over the scene of a lost campaign.

On February 8 the Japanese landed on Singapore Island, and the Argylls were at once in action alongside their Australian comrades. Forty-eight hours later they found themselves alone and cut off two miles in advance of the British lines. Painfully they fought their way back across country. Many are the stories told of the heroism of those desperate days of which one, which was widely reported, must suffice:

> 'A detachment of the regiment, after covering the retreat of the British and Indian troops was cut off with little chance of escape. The last job given to them was to hold the pipe-line. Three of them, ragged, exhausted and sun-tanned, made their way through the British force holding another position. Told that the Argylls had been wiped out and advised to get some sleep inside the British lines, a corporal said: "If we are the last of the battalion, then I am the senior non-commissioned officer. My last order was to hold the pipe-line. If the Commanding Officer is alive, he will be expecting us there. If not, he will expect us to hold the pipe-line." And all three turned back towards the enemy.'

As the battle for Singapore drew towards its inevitable conclusion their old Commanding Officer, Brigadier Stewart, gathered together a small party of two officers and about fifty men. They were black and greasy from fighting the fires at Kranji caused by the enemy bombing, and utterly exhausted. Brigadier Stewart reminded them of two promises he had made to them in the confident days before the war. One was never to put them into battle with in-sufficient fire power; the other was that, in adversity, he would never say to them 'Go on,' only 'Come on.' Brigadier Stewart writes:

> 'Now I told them I was going to break my promise; the first but the second remained. I did not order them, I asked – would they come into this last battle with me? There was no response, no audible one, only they quietly and determinedly got to their feet and stood waiting, all of them, and the march back to the fighting line began.'

In the event they never got there. Higher Command considered that nothing more should be asked of their gallant men and the order to withdraw was given. A few hours later it was all over and the 2nd Battalion ceased to exist. For the survivors there followed grim years in a prisoner-of-war camp, but their morale never broke. They remained to the end proud, defiant and utterly unbowed.

The total eclipse of the 2nd Battalion came to an end in 1944 when the King ordered that the 15th Battalion of the regiment be re-constituted as the 2nd Battalion. Under this title they played an important part in the invasion of Europe. As part of the 15th Scottish Division under the command of Major-General Gordon MacMillan, who had been Adjutant of the 2nd Battalion in France during the Great War, they successfully broke out of the bridgehead in two brilliant operations first on the River Odon and later near Caumont and pursued the enemy across France and Belgium to the banks of the Rhine. They were in the first wave to cross in face of bitter opposition and pressed on to the last line of German resistance on the River Elbe. They lost 181 killed and 620 wounded, but they maintained the high reputation they had inherited from those who died in 1942.

*Argyll and Sutherland Highlanders advance through Holland in 1944.*

The war history of the 1st and 2nd Battalions has been given at some length. There were, however, nine Argyll battalions engaged in one capacity or another in the conflict. Space does not allow the story of all the other battalions to be told, but mention must be made of the record of the 7th Battalion commanded in the initial stages of the war in the desert by Lorne Campbell, who won the Victoria Cross and two D.S.O.'s.

The battalion was in the thick of the fighting from the early days in France, through the desert and Sicily, the Normandy landings and the Campaign in Europe, culminating in the Rhine Crossing and the final defeat of the enemy inside Germany. Few, if any, battalions saw so much fighting during the last war and there were few of the original battalion who were not killed, wounded or captured, so that the strength was turned over several times. Between October 1942 and the end of the war in Europe, their

*The reconstituted 2nd Battalion hitch a ride during the push through Holland in 1944. The 15th Battalion was re-formed as the 2nd Battalion after the loss of the latter in Singapore.*

'score' in awards for gallantry was one V.C., nine D.S.O.s, sixteen M.C.s, five D.C.M.s, twenty-nine M.M.s and one B.E.M. The 8th Battalion too gained their full quota of decorations winning between them one V.C., eight D.S.O.s, twenty-five M.C.s, two D.C.M.s, fifty-one M.M.s, eight O.B.E.s and four M.B.E.s. These two battalions, the 7th and 8th were original first-line T.A. units and remained an infantry throughout the war.

It is perhaps not surprising that they used to sing with pride when conditions were grim:

'Ye may talk aboot yer Gordons and yer gallant Forty-Twa,
Yer Silver-Streakit Seaforths and yer Camerons sae Braw,
But gi's me the tartan o' the lads who look sae fine,
The Argyll and Sutherland Highlanders – "The Thin
                                        Red Line." '

# *Chapter*
# 9
## *1945–1969*

FOLLOWING the end of the war, there was for a time some uncertainty about the future of the 1st Battalion. The armistice in Italy was followed almost immediately by the collapse of Germany, but the war in the Far East lingered on. At one time it was thought that the battalion would be sent there, but peace was signed before this could be affected. Instead they returned to Palestine, where they had been at the outbreak of hostilities.

By 1945 the role of the British in Palestine had considerably altered. The Arabs no longer posed a threat to the internal security. Instead, break-away movements of Jews, such as the infamous Stern gang, were seeking to achieve their ends by sabotage and assassination. There followed a period for the battalion of alternate boredom and sporadic activity. Guard duties were particularly onerous and for considerable periods freedom of movement was very much restricted. Every now and again a new outrage, such as the blowing up of the King David Hotel, would occur which would result in the security precautions being tightened yet again. There followed a series of skirmishes and some casualties caused by time-fused bombs until, in April 1947, the battalion returned to its headquarters in Jerusalem.

The year 1947 was eventful for the regiment as a whole. In the first place it was then that the War Office decided that the 2nd Battalion should be put into a state of 'suspended animation' – a situation which has continued ever since. In the second place, it was the year in which Her Royal Highness The Princess Elizabeth was appointed to be Colonel-in-Chief, followed shortly afterwards by her marriage to His Royal Highness, the Duke of Edinburgh, to which many members of the regiment had the honour of being invited. In the same year Her Royal Highness and her regiment received the Freedom of the Royal Burgh of Stirling.

On September 26 the Secretary of State to the Colonies announced to the General Assembly of U.N.O. that Britain agreed to the terminating of the Mandate in Palestine. There followed a further period of increased tension while both Arabs and Jews digested the proposition. When the policy of Partition was announced there was more

*General Sir Gordon MacMillan of MacMillan of Knap, K.C.B., K.C.V.O., C.B.E., D.S.O., M.C., D.L. From the painting by Leonard Boden.*

trouble between Arabs and Jews in which the battalion had to intervene. These erratic conditions continued until a truce was finally declared at the beginning of the following year. The Mandate was finally relinquished on May 15 and the battalion immediately left for home via Port Said. The last to leave Palestine was the Colonel of the Regiment, Lieutenant-General Gordon MacMillan who had been G.O.C. during the final fifteen months of the Mandate. As he embarked, the R.A.F. staged a fly-past in his honour. Two destroyers and a frigate altered course to steam by while their crews gave three cheers for the General. When he stepped ashore at Port Said, his own regiment was there for form a Guard of Honour.

The battalion remained in Egypt for two months before returning home to be stationed at Colchester. It was here that the final ceremony marking the demise of the 2nd Battalion took place. Whilst the term 'suspended animation' was used to describe the status of the battalion, it was, in fact merged with the 1st Battalion as, in the words of the Colonel of the Regiment:

> 'It was unthinkable that the traditions of the 93rd should be lost.'

Many of the traditions of the old 93rd have been adopted by the 91st and the Regimental Flag and all signs used by the battalion carry the figures of both 91st and 93rd.

The battalion were home scarcely a year before they were off on their travels again, this time to Hong Kong. On the way they called at Singapore, which must have revived poignant memories for Major Slessor and 19 other ranks who had served in the heroic campaign with the 2nd Battalion and now returned with the 1st.

The year which followed in Hong Kong and the New Territories was relatively uneventful. The role of the battalion was in support of the Civil Power but there was no emergency which could not be dealt with by the Police, with the consequence that the Argylls were able to concentrate on training and on preparing against the possibility of an invasion by Red China.

These conditions lasted for just over a year. In the meantime, the North Koreans had invaded South Korea, an invasion which at first overwhelmed the defendants while the Americans stationed in Japan rushed to their aid. The situation remained critical and, at the beginning of August, the British decided to commit two battalions of the 27th Brigade. Those selected were the 1st Argylls and their old comrades-in-arms from the 1914–18 war, the 1st Middlesex. They landed from H.M.S. *Ceylon* on August 29, 1950 and, the situation being little short of desperate, were at once rushed to their concentration area at Kyongsan.

The battalion was extremely fit and ready for battle so that within a few days they found themselves taking over a sector on the Naktong River where they were occupied with patrols to establish the enemy strength. On one of these patrols commanded by Captain C. N. A. Buchanan, they ran into a heavy concentration of North Koreans and sustained several casualties, including Captain Buchanan and his batman. He was so badly wounded that he could not be moved without endangering the rest of the patrol. He therefore ordered his sergeant to take the patrol back and leave himself and his batman behind. It was only when this was given as a direct order that the sergeant reluctantly obeyed. The two men were never seen alive again. The following year a search party came on their bodies. Captain Buchanan was awarded the American Silver Star for his gallant self-sacrifice.

It was shortly after this incident that the Allies took the offensive and the Argylls were given an objective to capture, known as Hill 282. This was achieved after some hard fighting, but it soon became apparent that the feature was overlooked on the flank by higher ground, Hill 388, from which the enemy could make life extremely difficult for our troops. It was decided therefore to attempt to capture it. Meantime shelling and mortar fire were taking their toll of the men occupying Hill 282 and it became urgent to evacuate the wounded – an extremely tricky operation.

Major Muir, the Second-in-Command of the battalion, made his way up with a stretcher party and arrived with the forward troops to find them in an extremely perilous situation. He rallied the survivors of the two forward companies, redistributed the ammunition and generally inspired the men to greater efforts. The position was hourly becoming more critical and it was decided to call for an air-strike again at Hill 388. Air recognition strips were put out and shortly after noon three friendly aircraft appeared on the scene. They circled the target but, to everybody's dismay, then attacked Hill 282 with napalm bombs and machine-gun fire. In a short time the hill crest became a blazing inferno and the small surviving force of 5 officers and 35 other ranks were forced back down the hill.

Major Muir, however, refused to accept retreat and rallying his pathetically small force, led an assault back up to the still-burning crest against a hail of small arms fire. There he continued to cheer on his men with no regard for his own safety. When all the ammunition was exhausted for the rifles he personally continued to resist, manning the two-inch mortar until two bursts of enemy machine-fire mortally wounded him. His last words were: 'The Gooks will never drive the Argylls off this hill.' For his great bravery he was posthumously awarded the Victoria Cross and the American Distinguished Service Cross. Virtually one whole company had been wiped out but the battalion continued to carry out its patrol duties in its weakened state.

Reinforcement, however, arrived in time for the battalion as part of the 27th Brigade to play another important part in the battle: no less than leading the pursuit of the enemy down the centre line of the advance. There followed some strenuous skirmishing during an advance in which they were constantly subjected to sniping and sudden attack. On the last day of October they enjoyed their first day of rest since the advance had started on the 15th and it must have looked very much as if hostilities were over. This hope would have been justified but for the unexpected arrival of well-equipped units of Chinese Communists, called 'volunteers' by their Government. This gave the enemy numerical superiority, but not control of the air. There followed a carefully controlled withdrawal punctuated by vigorous periods of action, notably when the battalion went to the rescue of C Battery of the 61st American Field Artillery Battalion. The following letter from the Commanding General of the 1st U.S. Cavalry Division shows how successful the battalion was:

'1. May I take this means of expressing the appreciation of myself and officers and men of my command for the timely and vigorous support you afforded on November 5, 1950.

2. Needless to say our situation was critical when the Argyll and Sutherland Highlanders arrived. As you know, our small arms ammunition was close to exhaustion and the enemy strength was increasing as their reinforcements came in. To watch your men advancing to our relief was a most welcome and heartening sight.

3. This was the first opportunity my command has had to work with the British and you would have enjoyed hearing the favourable comments of my men during and after the action. They were greatly impressed by the discipline, coolness and workmanship of the British under fire. The British will always have strong supporters in this battalion.

4. Please express the thanks of this battalion to your command and may I hope that we may again be giving the privilege of serving with you.'

It was soon to become apparent what effect the intervention of the Chinese was to have on the fortunes of 27th

Brigade who might otherwise have expected to be back in their home station by Christmas. Instead they found themselves committed to a full winter campaign in sub-zero temperatures with no other protection than battledress.

There followed a very confusing time during which the Argylls came temporarily under command of the 7th U.S. Cavalry Regiment and formed the rearguard for a withdrawal of the United Nations forces. Later they rejoined their brigade and the withdrawal continued. At the end of the year they learned that the 27th Brigade had gained the award of the Presidential Unit Citation which entitled all members of the Brigade to wear the Presidential Citation Ribbon. New Year was celebrated in the Sergeants' Mess to the sound of enemy gunfire.

January 1 saw the resumption of the withdrawal, a process which was not reversed until the beginning of February when a slow methodical advance began. The main problem was to keep the forward units supplied as communication became very stretched. There was, however, little fighting as the Chinese had generally withdrawn from their strongholds before the arrival of our troops. The Argylls led the advance until the middle of March and then, after ten days in reserve, resumed their role for what was to be their last action in Korea. Shortly afterwards they embarked for Hong Kong to the accompaniment of messages of appreciation from all sides.

Whilst in Hong Kong they received the sad news of the death of His Majesty King George VI. Later the Colonel of the Regiment, Lieutenant-General Sir Gordon MacMillan received the following message from the Military Secretary:

'I am directed to inform you that The Queen has been graciously pleased to signify her willingness to continue as Colonel-in-Chief of your Regiment.'

Events in Korea had been closely followed by the public at home so when, on September 23, 1952, the battalion arrived back in Glasgow, it was received with no ordinary welcome. As one hardened docker remarked: 'I've seen many homecomings, but this is one I'll never forget.' There was a special message from the Queen, an official welcome from the Lord Provost, bands playing and streets lined with cheering crowds. Later it was all repeated in Edinburgh where Princes Street was closed to traffic and a huge crowd jammed it from end to end, with every window and balcony occupied and even people perched precariously on the roof tops.

These demonstrations were followed by a civic reception in Stirling and later the granting of the Freedom of Dunoon. The citation for this latter event read as follows:

'We, Edward Francis Wyett, Provost, Charles Macdonald Black and Alfred Campbell Morrison, bailies and remanent Councillors of the Burgh of Dunoon, in recognition of the outstanding services rendered by the Regiment to this Country and the Empire in many arduous campaigns and in particular recognition at this time of the brilliant Military achievements and resolute gallantry of the First Battalion in Korea, and also in proud acknowledgement of the Historical association existing between the County Battalion and this Burgh, do hereby confer on you the freedom of entry into the Burgh of Dunoon on ceremonial occasions with bayonets fixed, drums beating and Colours flying.'

There followed a round of ceremonial duties and the battalion was just beginning a training exercise the following year when an urgent message was received by dispatch rider ordering them back to camp. They were off on their travels again – this time to British Guiana.

It was at first feared that the position in British Guiana might deteriorate to a point where troops would have to intervene as a result of the activities of the quasi-Communist People's Progressive Party. The role of the battalion was to maintain friendly relations with the civilian population but, at the same time, to be alert for sudden trouble. In the event the fears proved unfounded and relationships rapidly improved with the result that a very pleasant year was spent in a wide variety of military and social activities. The battalion arrived back at Southampton on November 2, 1954.

They were not to stay at home for long. Within two months they were off to Berlin where they performed garrison duties for a year and a half. They returned to Bury St. Edmunds in August 1956. Within three months a state of emergency was once again declared and the battalion was sent with the 19th Brigade to Port Said to take control of the area following the Suez crisis. This proved to be an

*A look-out post in Aden, 1967.*

*Pipe-Major Robson leading the advance to re-take Crater, July 3–5, 1967.*

unpleasant operation but fortunately no casualties were suffered. The most dangerous period was during the withdrawal, following relief by U.N.O. troops. The Egyptians took to sniping and hit-and-run forays against our troops, and the battalion was charged with sending policing patrols into the worst areas like Shanty Town. The withdrawal went according to plan and the battalion arrived back in the U.K. on New Year's Eve, 1956.

During the next ten years the battalion was kept thoroughly occupied. After two years' training at home they were sent for the next year and a half to control the terrorists in Cyprus where they won great praise for their steadiness and calmness under great provocation. From Cyprus they went for another tour of duty in Germany, followed by five years at home, broken by a tour of duty in Singapore with incursions into Borneo. Then, in June 1967, they were sent to the latest place of crisis – Aden.

So much has been written about the Crater and the Argylls in recent times that there can be very few who do not know the main outline of the campaign. Rather than go into great detail here, a quotation from *The Thin Red Line*, the Argyll's Regimental Magazine, is given which clearly shows the reaction of the man on the spot to events which aroused world-wide interest and controversy.

'It is not often that one has the impression that one is at a milestone in Regimental History. These notes were written during the withdrawal from the Crater and the return of the battalion to Plymouth.

'There can be no doubt in the minds of any of us that the battalion did a good job in Aden. Crater *is* Aden in the minds of the South Arabians and the domination of the Crater from the re-entry on the 3rd July, through the period of attrition throughout July and August, into the period of comparative peace from September onwards, was undoubtedly a major factor in the negotiation of a final acceptable, if macabre, political solution. Our success in the Crater was achieved because the battalion, from the Commanding Officer to the latest joined Jock, had trained hard and realistically, knew what it was on and, collectively, had more general operational experience than any other battalion in the British Army. Good emerged from tragedy because, unlike other units, the battalion never had a handover of its operational area . . . and therefore never mirrored previous tactics or procedures but used brains, backed by resolution, to tackle every event and individual incident as it occurred.

'There is a tendency in the British Army to abide

slavishly by principles and procedures long after they are irrelevant. Aden was no exception. The Green Pamphlet on Internal Security postulates four guiding principles which may be excellent in a true I.S. situation. But it was clear from the moment the Advance Party arrived that the situation in Aden was not I.S. It was counter-terrorism. The Green Pamphlet, excepting minor tactical procedures, was therefore largely irrelevant. Fortunately the battalion had trained against a background of the Commanding Officer's seven principles which were: Supervision, Self Control, Offensive-Mindedness, Quick and Accurate Shooting, Well Tried Operational Drills, Intelligent Interest and Security Consciousness.

'The Tactical lesson of Aden was that these seven principles were the right ones.

*Major-General F. C. C. Graham, C.B., D.S.O., D.L., the present Colonel-in-Chief of the Regiment, who commanded the 1st Battalion through the Italy campaign, and his three sons who all served in the Regiment, two with the Regular Battalion and one with a Territorial Battalion.*

'The domination of the Crater was not achieved without cost. Our casualties in Aden, five killed and twenty-four wounded, were higher than those suffered by the battalion during Suez, Cyprus and Borneo combined. The death of Major Bryan Malcolm and Privates Moores and Hunter, who were tragically murdered on the 20th June, gave a crusader spirit to the reoccupation of the Crater. The lives of Corporal Scott and Private Orr were the price the battalion paid for controlling the Crater. These five are our real heroes, and it is at this time when the rest of us are returning to our families for Christmas and the New Year, that we all remember with sympathy those who are not so fortunate.

'One feature of our everyday life in Crater was our continual contact with the Press. Six months ago many of us probably looked upon a journalist or TV cameraman with suspicion. No Argyll who was in Aden now has this attitude. The Press Corps are all first-class chaps with an important job of work to do. We had the story they wanted and we did our best to give it to them. Every Jock became a professional TV subject, acting naturally and avoiding looking at the camera. We found that it was best to tell all, to show and explain everything to the Press. On the rare occasions when there was something that we would rather the Press should not publish, we found that they played ball and our confidence was never misplaced. However, there are exceptions to everything. Whilst none of us would criticise the accuracy of the reporting of the journalists and correspondents who were there and saw for themselves, it is noticeable that the truth is rarely in the armchair commentator who stays at home.'

The battalion returned to England proud of a job well done and their thoughts turned towards the future. Although as the author of the extract quoted above remarks, they could lay claim to being the most highly trained and experienced unit in the British Army, they were not content

A.S.H.—9*

to rest on their laurels as another paragraph from *The Thin Red Line* shows:

> 'Our unofficial motto "Get Up and Go" does not leave too much room for reminiscing. We return to Plymouth after leave on the 4th January and our attention will be focused on the future. Initially this will mean individual training, cadres and courses necessary to bring our individual skills up to the highest possible standard. After a few weeks of this we shall be on Company Training – Stanford, PTA, and Argyllshire and then, in the autumn, we hope to go to Kenya for two months' Battalion Training. We have plenty to do and much to look forward to. We have shown our worth to the Army and the Nation in Aden and elsewhere. Our country's enemies have a healthy fear of us. Our next campaign is the Battle for Survival, to win it we need more first-class recruits, mentally tough and physically sound young Jocks, to whom we can promise a challenging and active life in a most go-ahead Battalion.'

A few short months after the above was written, the blow fell. It was announced that with new defence cuts, the Argylls were to be disbanded. Possibly no regiment had captured the public imagination so completely since the days of the Thin Red Line than their heirs, the Argyll and Sutherland Highlanders, and the outcry at the news was loud and sustained. A million individuals signed a petition for a reprieve and stickers appeared everywhere in aid of the 'SAVE THE ARGYLLS' campaign.

As these words are being written the 1st Battalion are setting out for yet another tour abroad, this time to Berlin, but there is no sign of authority relenting. There is still time for a change of heart before 1971, the date set down. Meantime, for the gallant Argylls, it is a case of 'Business as Usual'.

*Stirling Castle, home of the Regiment since its creation in 1794.*

# *The Regimental March*

## THE THIN RED LINE.
### MARCH.

SOLO B♭ CORNET.

KENNETH J. ALFORD.

Trio.

Allargando.

*Sole Selling Agents:* BOOSEY & HAWKES, Ltd. 295 Regent Street, London. W.1. All rights reserved. Printed in England

## HIGHLAND LADDIE
### (Arranged for Bagpipes)

# THE CAMPBELLS ARE COMING
(Arranged for Bagpipes)

# The Argyll and Sutherland Highlanders
## 1794–1969

### 91st Argyllshire Regiment

| | |
|---|---|
| 1794 | Raised by Duncan Campbell of Lochnell |
| 1795–1802 | Cape of Good Hope |
| 1808–1815 | Peninsular War |
| 1822–1831 | Jamaica |
| 1836–1840 | St. Helena |
| 1842–1845 | South Africa |
| 1846–1848 | Kaffir War |
| 1851–1854 | Ireland |
| 1854–1858 | Mediterranean |
| 1858–1868 | India |
| 1879 | Zulu War |

### 93rd Sutherland Highlanders

| | |
|---|---|
| 1799 | Raised by Major-General William Wemyss |
| 1806–1814 | Cape of Good Hope |
| 1814–1815 | Campaign of New Orleans |
| 1815–1823 | Ireland |
| 1826–1834 | West Indies |
| 1838–1848 | Canada |
| 1854–1856 | Crimean War |
| 1857–1859 | The Indian Mutiny |
| 1860–1870 | India |

### The Argyll and Sutherland Highlanders

| | |
|---|---|
| 1881 | The 91st Argyllshire Highlanders and the 93rd Sutherland Highlanders were amalgamated to form the Argyll and Sutherland Highlanders |
| 1897 | Tochi Valley |
| 1899–1902 | South African War |

| 1914–1918 | The Great War |
| 1924–1925 | Sudan |
| 1929–1932 | Shanghai/Hong Kong |
| 1935 | Mohmand Operation |
| 1937 | Waziristan Operation |
| 1939–1945 | Second World War |
| 1945–1948 | Palestine |
| 1947 | 1st and 2nd Bns Amalgamated |
| 1949 | Hong Kong |
| 1950 | Korea |
| 1953–1954 | British Guiana |
| 1956 | Suez Operation |
| 1957–1959 | Cyprus |
| 1964–66 | Borneo |
| 1967 | Aden |